ERNEST HEMINGWAY
and his world

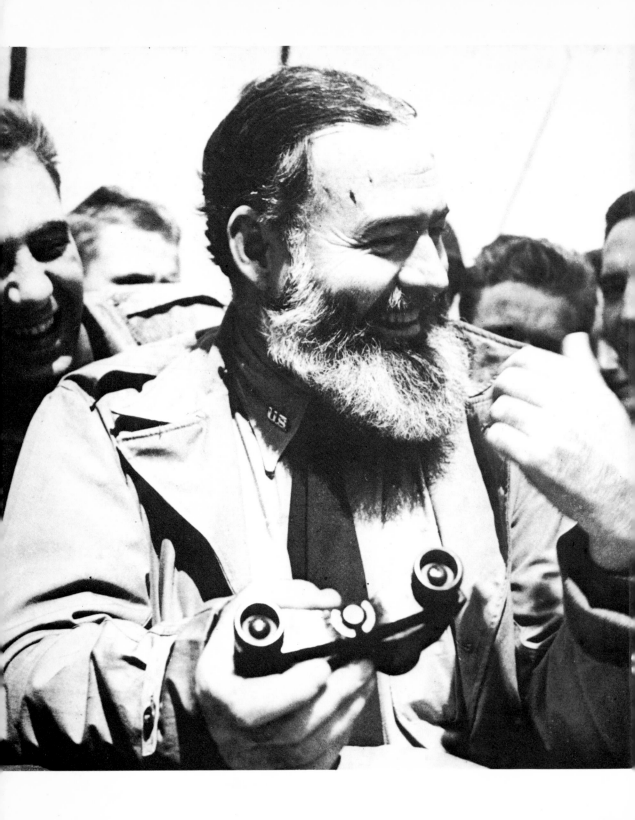

ANTHONY BURGESS

ERNEST HEMINGWAY

and his world

CHARLES SCRIBNER'S SONS
NEW YORK

Literature at Princeton University, of whom I was once a lowly and disregardable colleague. Though Hemingway himself spoke once with scorn (or is said to have so spoken) of Baker's scholarly appetite for the facts, that rigid concern with the biographical truth has served Hemingway better than the adoring memoir of A. E. Hotchner (on which, nevertheless, I have drawn once or twice). Hemingway the legend is treated sceptically by Professor Baker, but the portrait of Hemingway the man that emerges does not diminish the writer, hunter, warrior, bullfight aficionado. I acknowledge with gratitude the help I have received from Carlos Baker's nine hundred close pages and recommend his *Ernest Hemingway* unreservedly to any who wish to pursue the story beyond the limits allowable in a sketch as brief as my own.

I wish also to pay tribute to a book written by another old colleague of mine – Professor Arthur Waldhorn of the City College of New York. His *A Reader's Guide to Ernest Hemingway* is the most useful brief critical survey of the Hemingway œuvre that I know, and it has influenced in a salutary way the somewhat naïve view of Hemingway that I carried with me from boyhood to the point of undertaking this short biography. There are many other books on Hemingway, man or work or both, and I duly acknowledge at the end those I have read and found valuable. But it would be unjust if I did not, here and now, voice thanks to two genuine scholars from one ungenuine – even though he flaunted the plumes of Visiting Senior Fellow at Princeton and, in New York, that of Distinguished Professor.

A.B.
Monaco

2 July 1977

6

IF THE AUTHOR of *The Sun Also Rises* and *A Farewell to Arms* and *The Old Man and the Sea* and the Nick Adams stories had been an undersized weed, asthmatic or phthisic, living out strong-man fantasies in the literature he produced, he would still be one of the great American writers. But he was no weed. He was six feet tall, huge-chested, handsome, ebullient, a warrior, a hunter, a fisherman, a drinker. It is the fusion of sensitive and original artist and big-muscled man of action that has made of Ernest Hemingway one of the large international myths of the twentieth century. The myth is rendered intriguing and compelling through the presence, in personality and art alike, of an ambiguous attitude towards life and death, of a self-doubt which seems to contradict the positive stances assumed in war and on safari, of a genuine morbidity whose roots are knotty and resistant to the digger. But the two major aspects of the public Hemingway, the Hemingway of anecdote, canned-beer advertisement, bestseller list, sophomore course in American fiction, represent a junction of parental genes and temperaments.

One need not trouble to trace the ancestors of Hemingway back to their ports of landing on the Atlantic seaboard of North America. Both sides of the family were Anglo-Saxon, moderately prosperous, churchgoing, patriotic, undistinguished though worthy. His father was Clarence Edmonds Hemingway, usually known as Ed, a medical practitioner of Oak Park, Illinois, who had graduated at Oberlin and Rush Medical College, Chicago, a son of a Civil War veteran who had done well out of real estate in the Windy City. Ed Hemingway was black-bearded, big-shouldered, six feet tall, a lover of hunting, fishing, taxidermy, snake-pickling, campfire cookery. He not only handed on to Ernest a blacksmith's physique but gave him a

Ernest Hemingway's father, Dr Clarence Edmonds Hemingway. 'I am so pleased and proud you have grown to be such a fine big manly fellow', he wrote to Ernest in 1915.

On Sat mama and I went across
the ford at the river It is very
much higher.
I got six clames in the river
And some weat six feet tall
you loving son
Ernest m Hemingway

woodsman's training. Ed Hemingway had first a cottage, later a forty-acre farm, in the Michigan woods and, only seven weeks after his birth on 21 July 1899, Ernest was taken on his first visit to the American wilds. It was a strenuous journey: train from Oak Park to Chicago, horse cab to the Lake Michigan pier, steamer to Harbor Springs, narrow-gauge train to Petoskey, branch line to Bear Lake, rowing boat to the cottage called Windemere (Ernest's mother's tribute to ancestral waters, but an 'r' got lost). He was to make the journey often.

Ed Hemingway taught his boy fishing, the handling of tools and weapons, the cooking of venison, raccoon, squirrel, opossum, wild pigeon, lake fish. There must be no killing for killing's sake – a rule that Hemingway abandoned in his manhood. If you kill a thing you must eat it, said his father. So the boy Ernest had to chew away at a rank and leathery porcupine he had wantonly shot. The habit of lying, or romancing, about his outdoor prowess began when he was not quite five. He told his grandfather Hall that he had stopped a runaway horse singlehanded. The old man said that with an imagination like that he would end up either famous or in jail.

Ernest Hall ran a wholesale cutlery business in Chicago. He was a godly man, given to family prayers, and, like his son-in-law's father, a Civil War veteran, even something of a hero. But – and this was a foible he did not pass on to his grandson – he would never allow war to be discussed in his presence. Ernest Hemingway's middle name – Miller – came from a great-uncle who manufactured bedsteads. There was metallic commerce, woodsman's skill and Christian piety for him to inherit, but not much literature. On the other hand there was music, represented by his mother. Grace Hall – whom Ed

Opposite: The infant Ernest, with his parents and sister Marcelline – eighteen months his senior – and the family summer home of Windemere, Bear Lake, 1901.

Above: Grace Hall Hemingway, Ernest's mother – pious, sentimental but a good musician. The Hemingway ear for tone and rhythm came from her, as also the defective vision.

Above left: The second page of a letter written by Hemingway at the age of nine – 19 October 1908; the 'M' stood for Miller.

Family pictures. *Opposite:* The Hemingways in 1909. *Above:* Ernest at eighteen months. *Above right:* Ernest and Marcelline, dressed alike by a mother Hemingway was later to call an old bitch, in the garden of the house on Oak Park Avenue.

Hemingway met when they were fellow-students at Oak Park High School – was a very English-looking girl, blue-eyed, ample-bodied, fresh-complexioned. In her youth she looked out to a bigger world than Oak Park, possessing as she did a fine contralto voice and having been urged by her mother and her teachers to take up grand opera as a career. But scarlet fever had weakened her eyes and, when she made her singing debut at Madison Square Gardens in New York, she was put into considerable pain by the glare of the footlights. So she went back to Oak Park and married young Dr Hemingway. On North Oak Park Avenue she established herself as a music teacher and left the cooking to her husband. Ed, when calling on a patient, would sometimes telephone home to tell the hired girl to take the pie out of the oven. He was a notable pie-maker.

Grace Hemingway was given to pious sentimentality all her life and, as was to be expected, never cared much for her son's books. When Ernest was born she wrote in her diary: 'The robins sang their sweetest songs to welcome the little stranger into this beautiful world.' After his christening he was set down as 'an offering unto the Lord, to receive his name and henceforth to be counted as one of God's little lambs'. That lamb went astray as soon as it reached ramhood: Ernest's career may fancifully be seen as an over-reaction to the mother's boy image. When he was nine months old she dressed him in pink gingham with a floral hat, just like his sister Marcelline, who was

The Hemingway children at 600
North Kenilworth Avenue – Ernest,
Madelaine ('Sunny'), Marcelline,
Ursula, Leicester and Carol.

eighteen months older. In later life, he spoke of his mother as an old bitch. He was also to turn against his father but only when, anticipating the son, he had shot himself in a state of depression. Ernest's loyalties were never easily given, and they were always easily withdrawn.

Tough and loud and pugnacious from the start, Ernest craved the punchbag of a younger brother, but he never got one until, in his teens, Leicester Clarence Hemingway came too late to be a foil or a companion. He grew up with four sisters – Marcelline, Ursula, Madelaine and Carol, all big handsome girls – and these were to exert a notable influence on his attitude to women. To the end it was observed that, in the company of women of his own generation, he instinctively assumed the kidding, bossy, easily cowable role of a brother. Even from his wives (also four, the first three sprung of a common mother, the city of St Louis) he demanded sisterly good-sport qualities. He wanted, but never achieved, a daughter, and he made filial surrogates out of pretty young women like Ava Gardner and Ingrid Bergman (though never of Marlene Dietrich: his attitude to her was interestingly complicated). He called them daughter and they had to call him papa. He became Papa Hemingway to everybody relatively early in life. Brotherly and fatherly enough, he was never much of a son.

He rejected his father's interest in science and, to some extent, resisted his mother's attempts to turn him into a musician. She wanted Ernest to become a professional violoncellist, and he did in fact play the easy 'cello parts of light operatic and musical comedy scores in his high-school orchestra. He also sang in the choir of the Third Congregational Church but, like his father, he was never able to carry a melodic line. In later life he claimed a fair knowledge of music and would even discourse (how learnedly has not been recorded) on counterpoint. In Paris he was to cause offence by saying of the music of George Antheil that he preferred his Stravinsky straight – a very clear-eared judgment on the 'bad boy of music', Ezra Pound's protégé, known now chiefly for his banal film scores. In Havana he made up a song for the voice and guitar consort of his favourite bar, and they would regularly discourse it whenever he came in. What he probably inherited from his mother was the concern with tone and rhythm that was to make him into a major literary stylist. Joyce too had a musical background. One can read neither *Ulysses* nor *A Farewell to Arms* without being aware of a preoccupation with words as sound, as well as a structural capacity analogous to that of a musical composer. Ernest's mother also had an eye for pictures and, in middle age, became a painter of regional reputation. The son's pictorial taste was to outclass the mother's, and, while he spoke of trying to do for a novel what Cézanne did for a canvas, critics invoked Goya in connection with some of his grimmer word-painting.

Ernest's career at grammar school and at the palatial Oak Park and River Forest Township High School was academically distinguished only for his achievement in English, and, at the end of it, he showed no inclination to move on to university. There was always a good deal of the anti-intellectual about him. He wrote stories and pieces of school-magazine reportage that, in their concern with the recording of physical action and their eschewing of romantic lexical display, foreshadowed his mature work. His main ambitions were athletic but, as a high-school freshman, he was ashamed of his lack of height and beef. Too small for football, he worked at rifle marksmanship and recorded a consistent score of 112 out of 150 at a twenty-yard range.

School days. Ernest attended Oak Park and River Forest High School (*right*). Its magazine was called *The Tabula*, its weekly newspaper *The Trapeze*. In the group photograph of *The Trapeze* staff (*above*), Marcelline and Ernest are to be seen on the front row, respectively third from the reader's left, second from his right.

Trapeze Staff

ASSOCIATE EDITORS

Elliott Smeeth	Earle Pashley
Ernest Hemingway	Le Roy Huxham
Susan Lowrey	Marcelline Hemingway

AIR LINE PILOT
Morris Musselman

CARTOONIST
Albert Dungan

REPORTERS

Arthur Thexton	Florence Winder
Allen Speelman	Edward Andresen
Laura Canode	Helen Sinclair
Fred Wilcoxen	Raymond George
Franklin Lee	Annabel Marchant
Helen Carr	Ray Ohlsen
Jack Pentecost	Clarence Savage

FACULTY ADVISORS

Business...Mr. Owen
Editorial...Mr. Gehlman

BUSINESS STAFF

Business Manager....................................Gordon Shorney
Assistant..Wilbur Brandt
Advertising Manager..............................Dale Bumstead
Assistants.........................Wiley Caldwell, Julian Lull

---

MADELEINE HANCOCK
Glee Club (3) (4); Opera (3); Atalanta (2) (3) (4); French Club (3) (4); Girls' Club (3) (4).

"As smooth as the business side of a banana peel."
WARD BELMONT

WILBUR HAUPT
Glee Club (2) (3); Opera (2); German Play (2); Athletic Association (4); Boys' High school Club (3) (4); Hanna Club (3).

"Cheeks like roses."
ILLINOIS

ERNEST HEMINGWAY
Class Prophet; Orchestra (1) (2) (3); Trapeze Staff (3), Editor (4); Class Play; Burke Club (3) (4); Athletic Association (1) (2) (4); Boys' High School Club (3) (4); Hanna Club (1) (3) (4); Boys' Rifle Club (1) (2) (3); Major Football (4); Minor Football (2) (3); Track Manager (4); Swimming (4).

"None are to be found more clever than Ernie."
ILLINOIS

MARCELLINE HEMINGWAY
Commencement Speaker; Orchestra (1) (2) (3) (4); Glee Club (3) (4); Tabula Board (4); Trapeze Staff (3), Editor (4); Opera (1) (2) (3); Atalanta (2) (3) (4); Girls' Rifle Club (2) (3) (4); Commercial Club (4); Drama Club (4); Girls' Club (3), Council (4); Story Club (3).

"I'd give a dollar for one of your dimples, Marc."
OBERLIN

This was in spite of a defective left eye that he cursed as an inheritance from his mother, though he was later to blame it (being loath to accord his mother anything) on the filthy tactics of boxing opponents. He shot up suddenly at fifteen and soon attained his father's height and weight – as well as propensity for copious sweating and putting on fat. He became well known for large and clumsy feet, on football field and dance floor alike. He did not play football well, but he ran, boxed, swam, and was made captain of the water basketball squad. And, of course, he wrote.

His model was Ring Lardner, who produced a popular column in the *Chicago Tribune* and had developed a mock-illiterate style that Ernest sought to imitate. Lardner's skill was greater than appeared on the surface; his medium was an original, though very American, invention – funny, subtle, capable of quiet pathos. Ernest was merely facetious, but facetiousness was a prized aspect of provincial American

A Vanity Fair caricature of Ring Lardner, 1925. Hemingway had been billed as 'OUR RING LARDNER, JR' in *The Trapeze*.

15

utterance in those days (Sinclair Lewis's *Babbitt* is probably the ultimate compendium). Wit was a product of intellect, and intellect was suspect, being European and decadent and ungodly. Facetiousness came out at its most excruciating in nicknames. Hemingway was a great nickname man, calling his little brother Leicester de Pester after a comic-strip character, liking himself to be called Porthos, Butch, the Old Brute, and, best of all, Hemingstein. There is a whiff of anti-semitism here: all Jewish names are comic. He never got over subdued kike-baiting, as he never got over his fondness for being called Hemingstein. In the Second World War, as a variation, he would introduce himself to GIs as 'Ernie Hemorrhoid, the poor man's Pyle'.

Those were good expansive days in the Middle West, with huge steaks and baked Idahos, root beer, back-slapping, chauvinism and optimism. American neurosis had not yet set in, and the little old US was the best God-damn country in the whole God-damn world. Hemingway's Oak Park was a good deal more innocent than Joyce's Dublin, nor can we imagine the young Hemingway moaning through the night-time streets like a beast, desperately wanting a woman. He certainly yearned for certain girls and was later to boast of never failing to have a woman he wanted, but it is evident that he kept his virginity a great deal longer than Joyce did. The religiosity of the town kept children in ignorance of the facts of life. Even a professional medical man like Ed Hemingway was prepared to assert that masturbation was a sure way to madness. Oak Park was proverbially the place where the bars ended and the churches began. There were no loose ladies around and the high-school girls were respectable. Ernest's body, anyway, was dedicated to athletics in termtime and the great Michigan outdoors in the summer vacation. It was a good wholesome life, and very loud, but the time inevitably came when the young Hemingway wanted more than the call of the chipmunks and the constraints of happy but stuffy Oak Park.

On 6 April 1917, the United States broke two and a half years of peace-at-any-price neutrality and declared war on Germany. Many young men were eager to get over there – indeed, many were already there in ambulance units or, at least, up over the 49th Parallel in the Royal Canadian Flying Corps – but Ernest was in no hurry. He had an instinct about priorities, and he wanted to learn how to write before he was taught how to fight. Anyway, his father had authoritatively declared that that defective left eye would keep him out of combat. Ernest had an uncle – Tyler Hemingway – in Kansas City; he also had an admiration for the *Kansas City Star*, still one of the great newspapers of America. Hearing that his chances of becoming a cub reporter on it were good, he said goodbye to his father, who kissed him fondly at the railway depot, tears in his moustache and a prayer on his

Opposite below: The second Hemingway home – 600 North Kenilworth Avenue, Oak Park, wide enough for Grace's music at one end and Ed's laboratory tinkerings at the other. Ernest, like his father, also enjoyed out-of-door activities: here he is seen with nameless companions on a camping trip (*opposite above*) and posed as all-American apprentice woodsman on the shore of Walloon Lake, 1913 (*above*).

lips. Ernest fictionalized that little scene many years later in *For Whom the Bell Tolls*, making his hero feel 'suddenly so much older than his father and sorry for him that he could hardly bear it'.

To speak of the young Hemingway's possessing a 'literary ambition' would probably be false. Scott Fitzgerald, fresh from Princeton, was at this time working on Compton Mackenzie type fiction, garnished with Keatsian tropes, a book-writer from the start, but Hemingway was already possessed of an instinctive aim both simpler and more complex – to draw the aesthetic disposition of language away from its traditional locations in the head and heart and to attach it to the nerves and muscles. This meant a genuine revolution that, for the moment, disguised itself as a desire to work well in the simple popular medium of journalism. But to say that Hemingway's ambition was to be a journalist would be as false as to say he wished to be a new Tolstoy or Dickens.

Kansas City is two cities. There is one in the state of Kansas, with a population of about 130,000, and another in the state of Missouri, with nearly half a million citizens. It is this latter which is usually meant when there is talk or song about Kansas City, and it was here that Ernest Hemingway started as a professional, or paid, writer. Today Kansas City is an elegant centre of trade and culture, with wide boulevards, much Spanish-style architecture, fine villas, restaurants in which mannequins exhibit the *haute couture* while the best beefsteaks in the world are served, a great Jesuit college, and a sumptuous hotel that incorporates a whole hillside, with trees and a running stream, into its décor. In 1917 it was a growing town whose tough frontier status was still a living memory, full of sin and crime and a cynical attitude to the law even among the magistrates, and its Twelfth Street had so many prostitutes that it was nicknamed Woodrow Wilson Avenue (a piece at any price). Ernest did not engage in either brawls or bought dalliance; he was a mere observer of the world of tough action. He was given fifteen dollars a week and a copy of the *Star* style-book which, in effect, told him to write in the style of the mature Hemingway. Brevity, a reconciliation of vigour with smoothness, the positive approach (say what is there rather than what is not there) – these were the *Star* rules. It was his later task to adapt them to the making of literature.

There was no shortage of material on the reporter's beat for depositing in the bank, later, with the interest of imaginative insight accrued, to be dispensed as Hemingway fiction. The remarkable story 'God Rest You Merry, Gentlemen', for instance, draws on something Ernest heard of on one of his regular trips to the City Hospital – the strange case of the youth who had, like the Church father Origen, castrated himself for the love of God. The impairment, physical or psychological, of sexuality evidently fascinated Hemingway: there was

The young Ernest as fisherman in the wilds of Michigan. His later catches were satisfyingly larger.

Mae Marsh as 'the little sister' in D. W. Griffith's film *The Birth of a Nation*.

The dubious attractions of Europe – and the First World War. A casualty (*opposite above*) and encampments (*below*) on the Italian front, where Hemingway was soon to see action.

undoubtedly something in himself that feared sexual commitment. But in general he discovered that real life always outdoes fiction; literature is not primarily invention: it is the ordering into aesthetic patterns of the *données* of a wide-ranging experience.

Kansas City showed him life, but he soon began to hunger for the bigger life of Europe at war, life with danger and death in it. Ted Brumback, a fellow cub, had not merely a weak eye but a glass one, and yet he had spent four months in the American Field Service, driving ambulances in France. Fired by this precedent, Ernest drew his last pay from the *Star* on the last day of April 1918, and was in May swaggering along Broadway, Manhattan, in the uniform of an honorary second lieutenant. He was in the Red Cross and was never to be officially a combatant in any war, but the myth of Hemingway the warrior was not slow now to come into existence. He wrote thumping lies to his friends in Kansas City, boasting that he was having an affair with Mae Marsh, star of *The Birth of a Nation*, and had sunk the 150 farewell plunks donated by his Pop on an engagement ring. He genuinely saw President Wilson and even, as right guide to his platoon in a parade of 75,000, marched down Fifth Avenue in his honour. His letter-style is excruciatingly ebullient: 'Ha Ha Ha Ha Ha Ha! Tis none other than the greatest of the Hemingsteins that indicts this epistle.' Soon, on a ship of the French line called the *Chicago*, a touch of welcome or homage that pleased him, he was on his way to the war and a diminution of his Middle West innocence.

He was taken, via Bordeaux and Paris and the Mount Cenis tunnel, to Milan. On his very first day there, he and his fellow ambulance men were hurled into the horror of the war when a munition factory exploded and they had to pick up bodies and pieces of bodies – mostly of women. It was a profound shock to a young innocent who had slain more than his share of small harmless animals but had never before met human death, let alone death on such a scale and of such gratuitous obscenity. On his third day he was sent, in a group of twenty-five, to Schio in the Dolomites. The war was going on over the hills, and there were many Italian wounded to be evacuated. At Dolo Hemingway met John Dos Passos, another Chicago man doing ambulance work and destined, in the view of Jean-Paul Sartre, to be the greatest American novelist of them all. Neither seems, at this first of many meetings, to have caught the other's name. The Austrians were attacking all along the Piave, north of Venice, and on the west bank the Italians were digging in. Volunteers were required to man the Red Cross canteens in the small towns behind the lines, and Ernest – who, as they said in Kansas City, always wanted to go where the action was – got himself sent to Fossalta, a much-punished village on the river.

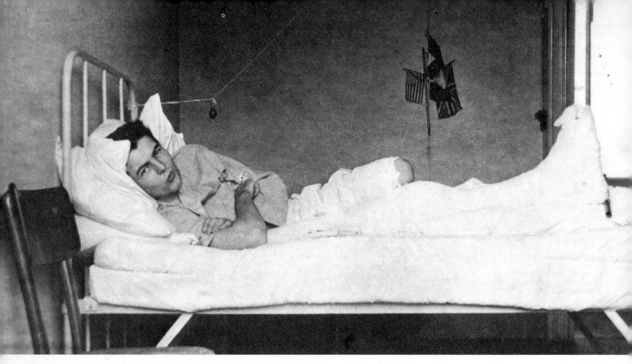

The consequences of war for a
lieutenant in the Red Cross:
discomfort – in the Ospedale Croce
Rossa Americana (*above top*) and on
crutches (*opposite*); and love – Sister
Agnes Hannah von Kurowsky
(*above*), first choice from eighteen
nurses.

One hot and moonless night he bicycled to a forward command
post and, helmeted and crouching against the crossfire, took cigarettes
and chocolate to the men in the trenches. Soon after midnight the
Austrians hurled a projectile across the river – a five-gallon canister
crammed with scrap metal – and many Italians were hit. Ernest picked
up a man who was crying in agony and, in a fireman's lift, tried to get
him towards the command post. After about fifty yards an Austrian
machine gun tore into his left leg. He fell, recovered, and made the final
hundred yards with his still-living burden. Then he lost consciousness.
His tunic was so soaked in blood – that of the man he had saved – that
the stretcher-bearers at first thought he had been hit in the chest. He
was taken to a shed where so many lay dead or dying that, so he said
later, it seemed to him more natural to die than to go on living. After
two hours he was taken to an emergency medical post at Fornaci,
where twenty-eight of the hundreds of fragments lodged in his leg were
removed. At length he was removed to the place he had started from
six weeks before – the Ospedale Croce Rossa Americana, on the Via
Alessandro Manzoni in Milan. There were eighteen nurses for only
four patients. Hemingway's war was over, though he expressed eager-
ness to get back into it as soon as his leg was well. He was a hero. He
had been recommended for the Italian medal of valour. He was young
and handsome, he breathed the powerful sexuality of the war-
wounded. He had eighteen nurses to fall in love with, and he fell
desperately for Sister Agnes Hannah von Kurowsky, a dark-haired
beauty from Washington, DC.

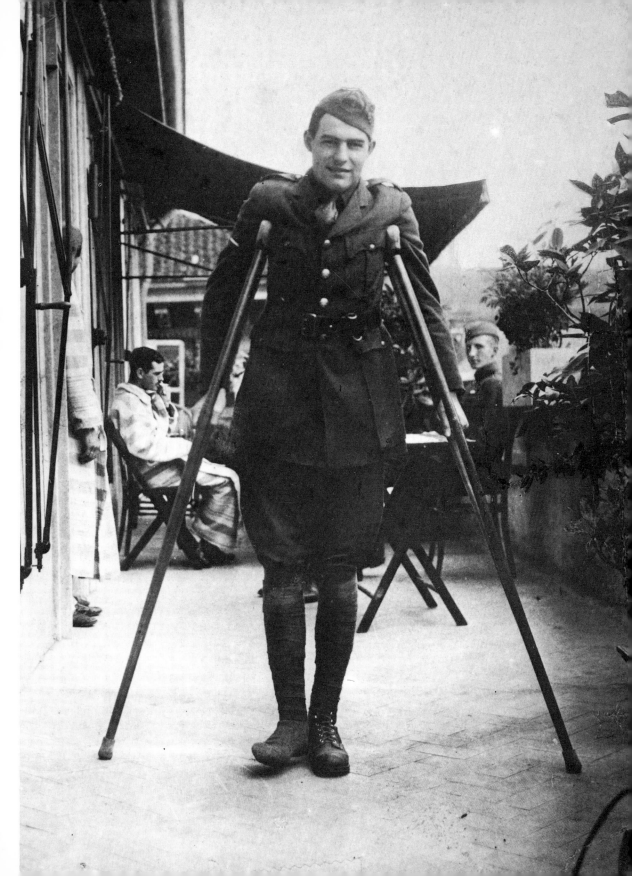

The returned hero, complete with Italian cloak, in Oak Park, 1918.

Opposite: Michigan Avenue, Chicago, looking north from the river. The Hemingway hometown was only a brief train ride away.

She responded with guarded affection but, being almost thirty, wished to avoid too deep an entanglement with a young man not yet twenty. That she found him attractive is well attested, and she was not the only one. Apart from the well-knit handsomeness, there was a maturity, a kind of authoritative vitality, that had been born out of danger. He had been tested under fire and not found wanting; he was learning about love; he was even developing a philosophy about death. He thought much about the grey-haired soldier of fifty-five he had met at the first-aid post who, when Ernest said 'You're *troppo vecchio* for this war, pop,' replied: 'I can die as well as any man.' He met Eric Dorman-Smith, OC British troops in Milan, who quoted something from *Henry IV Part Two* that was henceforth to be a kind of cantrip for Hemingway. It is Feeble, the 'woman's tailor', who, submitting to be pressed for the war by Falstaff, says: 'By my troth, I care not; a man can die but once; we owe God a death . . . and let it go which way it will, he that dies this year is quit for the next.'

The Italian war experience, the love for a Red Cross nurse, 'grace under pressure', contact with an older faith than he had met in his parents' Third Congregational Church in Illinois, wine and blood, the antiquity of Europe – such discoveries were slow to work towards the *Gestalt* of *A Farewell to Arms*, but they turned Ernest into a kind of European. He was never to write much about America, where, he said, nothing really happened; he returned to Oak Park dissatisfied, though fêted as a hero. He mooned around in his Italian military cloak, drank *vino*, sang old songs of the Piave, did nothing about looking for work. His very speech had changed. He had picked up a clipped manner of delivery from Dorman-Smith, and this went well with his chronic lambdacismus (an inability to pronounce the lateral consonant, so that lilies in his mouth were wiwwies). He dreamed of Agnes and wrote to her every day, but it soon became clear that she had fallen in love with a handsome young Neapolitan. Ernest was in a black rage for a time. Nothing, however, had really been lost. He was not likely to confuse love henceforth with mere *Schwärmerei*; a book would come out of it some day. Meanwhile, kicked out of the house by his mother, who complained of his layabout habits, he took lodgings in Chicago. There he wrote pieces for the magazine section of the *Toronto Star*, and he looked vainly for a market for his short stories.

In the fall of 1920, a girl named Elizabeth Hadley Richardson came to Chicago from St Louis, Missouri, to stay with friends for a time, being weary from the ordeal of her mother's long illness and slow death. At parties she met many boisterous young men, among them one who was variously called Ernie, Nesto, Oinbones, Wemmedge, Hemmy, Stein, Hemingstein. They found each other attractive. She was eight years his senior, with auburn hair and a tall and graceful

Elizabeth Hadley Richardson, the first Mrs Ernest Hemingway.

Opposite above: The wedding day, 9 March 1921. Of wedding gifts Hemingway wrote:

Three travelling clocks
Tick
On the mantelpiece
Comma
But the young man is starving.

This was a slight exaggeration.

Opposite below: Sherwood Anderson, who advised the newly married couple to go to Paris.

figure. She knew little of life; she looked up to the white-toothed war hero with a talent for writing and anecdote. Her Chicago nickname was Hash, but he called her Hadley. He visited her when she returned to St Louis, and she was only too eager to come back to Chicago for the bright lights and talk about how lousy America was and the only place to be was Europe. Soon they talked of marriage, but Ernest's financial prospects were thin. He had tried and then abandoned a novel; he could not sell his short stories; he had only forty dollars a month from editing a Cooperative Movement magazine that he had to write almost entirely by himself and that was run by crooks anyway. Hadley had a small trust fund that brought in $3,000 a year. Like many a struggling artist before and after him, Ernest was prepared to live on a woman until his breakthrough came. They married. Soon, they said, they were going to go to Italy to live.

No, said Sherwood Anderson, not Italy. Make it Paris, the only place for a writer. Anderson was a known and respected author in

Paris in the twenties: the Café du Dôme.

early middle age, best known now for his *Winesburg, Ohio*. He became a stylistic influence on the young Hemingway, who was, however, quick not only to reject him but even to satirize him. At the moment Anderson was living with his wife Tennessee in a Chicago suburb, having escaped from the particular oppressiveness of the philistine Middle West society he was attacking in his fiction, but aware that the whole of America was filled with a go-getting materialistic euphoria that was the death of the soul. Go to Paris, he said, where art is taken seriously, where, in the words of Henry James, the very air is suffused with style. Hemingway found the *Toronto Star* willing to accept a series of Letters from Europe. He booked passages on the *Leopoldina*, whose Joycean name would soon seem to have been a good omen. Here, said Anderson, are letters of introduction – to Gertrude Stein the great expatriate American prose innovatrix, to Sylvia Beach who part-owns Shakespeare and Co., the bookshop in the rue de l'Odéon, to Ezra Pound the poet and writer's friend, to Lewis Galantière of the International Chamber of Commerce. In gratitude, the night before sailing, Hemingway put all his unused canned goods in a sack, humped them to Anderson's house, and clanked them on to the floor.

Left: James Joyce, poor but dapper, with Sylvia Beach outside Shakespeare and Co. The year is 1920; in two more years *Ulysses* will be published, in default of courageous commercial publishers, by Miss Beach herself.
Below: Joyce in discussion with her in the shop.

Gertrude Stein in Paris. An American expatriate prose experimentalist, she took the tyro Hemingway under her wing.

Hemingway had been boxing a good deal lately – chiefly as a sparring partner in order to earn a little money. On the ship he organized an exhibition bout to provide a few francs for a French girl who, abandoned by her doughboy husband, was going tearfully home. In Paris, almost the first thing he did was to propose a round or two to Lewis Galantière, who had called at their hotel to invite them to dinner. He broke Galantière's glasses. Everybody seems sooner or later to have been invited to a session with the gloves – save for the unfit, like Ford Madox Ford, the near-blind, like James Joyce, the wrong-sexed, like Gertrude Stein. He boxed all the time he was in Paris. It was an outward expression of the big inner fight that was going on – not a scrap with what a Jamesian novelist would regard as the major problems of literary creation – character, motivation, philosophical truth, architectonics – but a struggle to write a 'true simple declarative sentence'. Hemingway's artistic aim was as original as that of any of the avant-garde literati who expatiated in the boulevard cafés. To describe without frills, without the imposition of an attitude, making word and structure convey thought and feeling as well as physicality –

Joyce in 1934. Discouraged by severe eye trouble and intermittent blindness, he was pushing on with his last great revolutionary book, *Finnegans Wake*.

this sounds easy now, chiefly because Hemingway has shown us how to do it, but it was not easy at a time when 'literature' still meant fine writing in the Victorian sense, with neo-Gothic decoration, bookish allusions, an intricate structure of subordinate clauses, the personality of the writer coyly or brutally thrusting between the reader and the thing read about.

Gertrude Stein was one of the American expatriates who were trying to cleanse English, to administer aesthetic shocks (meaning to force readers to look at the external world as if for the first time) through a perhaps excessive simplification of language. Hemingway, young enough to be her son, humbly showed her his work – his fragment of a novel, free verse in Ezra Pound's 'imagist' style. Too much description for its own sake, she objected; too much decoration; compress, concentrate. James Joyce had, starting in Trieste, finishing here in Paris, already worked out his own stylistic salvation in *Ulysses* – a 'most goddamn wonderful book', said Hemingway when it appeared in 1922 – in which the old rhetoric is destroyed through mockery, the mind speaks directly in interior monologue, and the phenomena of the exterior world are caught with a sharp compression not then apparent to everybody. Ezra Pound, who had founded the new dialect of Anglo-American poetry in 1917 with his *Homage to Sextus Propertius* and had first brought Joyce to the notice of the international (i.e. Parisian) literary world, saw the talent of the young Hemingway. He gave him encouragement and, in return, he was given boxing lessons.

But it was Sherwood Anderson who first got Hemingway into the print of a literary journal. The journal was the New Orleans *Double Dealer*, and Hemingway's contribution was a satirical fable and four lines of verse – the lines printed to fill up a page that featured a long poem by William Faulkner, the Southern writer who was to create his own revolution in the American novel. Encouraged, Hemingway asked Hadley to bring all his manuscripts from Paris to Lausanne, where he was on an assignment for the *Toronto Star*, to see what else he could publish or polish with a view to publication. She left the suitcase full of manuscripts unattended for a moment in the train at the Gare de Lyon; she came back to find it gone. Hemingway's rage was intense: Hadley saw a frightening side of him that presaged an impairment of their union. He 'would almost have resorted to surgery in order to forget' the loss, he said later, but the calamity was perhaps a blessing: he was forced to start again from scratch.

In 1923 many of his pieces were accepted for publication. Margaret Anderson and Jane Heap were running a reputable magazine called *The Little Review*; Harriet Monroe edited *Poetry*: he was to appear in both. Moreover, Paris was not only the home of genuine writers and posing layabouts: it was also the centre of the American gentlemen publishers – men with money and a devotion to fine printing in limited editions – Harry Crosby, Robert McAlmon, William Bird, others. McAlmon, a Kansan married to Annie Winifred Ellerman, better known to literature as Bryher, wanted to bring out Hemingway's *Three Stories and Ten Poems*. Later, Bird was to publish *in our time* – a collection of stories and sketches whose lower-case title serves to distinguish it from Hemingway's first commercial publication, *In Our Time*.

Meanwhile, Hemingway reported back to Toronto about the turbulent unhappy Europe that was emerging out of the Peace. He sent cables not only from Paris but from Genoa, in whose slums the northern Italian Communist movement was fomenting, from Muradli and Adrianople and other firepoints of the Greco-Turkish war, from Constantinople, soon to be Istanbul and the capital of Kemal Ataturk's social revolution, from the Lausanne Peace Conference summoned in 1923 to settle the territorial disputes of the Balkans. He met Clemenceau, whose tigrine excoriation of Canada as a nation

John Dos Passos at Schruns, Austria, in the mid-1920s. Best known for his left-wing stylistically revolutionary trilogy *U.S.A.*, he has been regarded by Jean-Paul Sartre as the greatest novelist of the century.

insufficiently committed to the late war the *Star* refused to publish. He met Mussolini, 'the biggest bluff in Europe'. In Italy with Hadley he made the mistake of revisiting the past – 'chasing yesterdays is a bum show' – and at Schio he and John Dos Passos each learned who the other was. Don Passos was preparing a trilogy – *U.S.A.* – formally more experimental than anything Hemingway was to do, but crude in its explicit political partisanship. He leaned to Communism; Hemingway, despite *The Fifth Column* and *For Whom the Bell Tolls*, which belong to the Spanish Civil War period when every good man leaned to the Loyalists, never became a political writer, one aspect of his fictional strength. Though bombarded later by the American Left as a neutral hedonist, he clung fast to the writer's one right and duty –

The bug of bullfighting begins to bite. Hemingway at a *corrida* in Madrid, 1923. *Right:* Pamplona in the Basque country of Navarre. Each morning during the Fiesta of San Fermín, the bulls galloped over the cobbles to the Plaza de Toros, the young bucks of the town running before, playing with death.

Opposite:
The bulls entering the arena, a sight Hemingway claimed to have seen thousands of times. *Below:* The great torero, Nicanor Villalta.

to show things and people as they are, uncoloured by ideology. For all that, the political analyses of the European situation that he cabled to the *Star* were sophisticated enough, also sometimes prophetic. All his life he was to be ahead of the politically committed in his ability to see the emerging shapes of policies and régimes.

Hemingway paid his first visit to Spain not on any journalistic assignment but because he was curious: Iberia was the one Latin territory he did not know. He was impressed by a *corrida* he saw in Madrid and became convinced that bullfighting was a tragic ritual rather than a mere bloody sport. Back in Paris, he was urged by Gertrude Stein to visit Pamplona in Navarre for the July Fiesta of San

Fermín. Hadley was as eager to go as he. She was sick of the squalor of their Paris flat; she was restless; she was pregnant. He spoke of the invigorating influence of bullfights on children yet unborn. They went, they were fascinated, they were hooked. There were baroque religious processions, there was wine-swilling, dancing of the *riau-riau*, the early morning galloping of the dagger-horned Villar bulls through the cobbled streets with the laughing foolhardy young Pamplonans running before them. Hemingway became an aficionado *in excelsis*. He idolized the torero Nicanor Villalta; if they had a son, he was to be christened Nicanor Villalta Hemingway. He wrote little sketches of the bullfights, vigorous, gory, dispassionate rather than brutal. They were to go into *in our time*.

Books, then, were appearing, but they were slim stuff, arty, coterie fodder: the dignity and profit of a big book published by a big American house seemed far and unattainable. The McAlmon volume was certainly something to take back to America, whither – so that their child should not be born on foreign soil – Ernest and Hadley now had to return. Not the United States, but the Dominion of Canada, with Hemingway, broke, working on the *Toronto Star* as a harassed and bullied reporter considered too big for his boots (he had been showing the McAlmon book round the office) and, as a punishment from the new tough editor, deprived of by-lines. John Hadley Nicanor

35

Hemingway in the courtyard of his new Paris home in the rue Notre Dame des Champs, 1924. The only reason for writing journalism, the struggling writer said later in the year, was to be well paid.

Hemingway was duly born (perhaps, after all, the Villalta bit would have been going too far). Edmund Wilson – yet to be acknowledged as America's greatest literary critic – saw the worth of Hemingway's spare prose; Bird published *in our time*. The father, husband, struggling writer and former *Star* staffman who, in January 1924, set out once more for Paris, had troubles enough ahead of him, but he could not now be called a literary tyro.

They found an apartment over a sawmill and lumber yard on the rue Notre Dame des Champs, and they hired a *femme de ménage* who lived at 10 *bis*, Avenue des Gobelins. John Hadley Nicanor was given the nickname of Bumby. When he learned to talk, this was the address he was to give if ever he was lost.

John Hadley Nicanor, better known as Bumby, in Paris, 1924. *Above:* With his father. *Below:* With Gertrude Stein and her companion Alice B. Toklas.

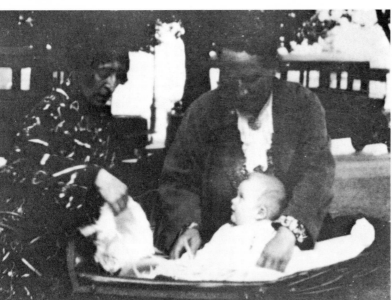

Dix bis Avenue des Gobelins,
Dix bis Avenue des Gobelins,
Dix bis Avenue des Gobelins,
That's where my Bumby lives.

(three times)

* This is how the song was sung to me by one who alleged he had sung it. The tune, right or wrong, will serve.

Above: Ford Madox Ford, great editor and author of the masterpieces *The Good Soldier* and *Parade's End.* Paris, 1923

Right: It was Hemingway's achievement, acting as deputy editor, to get Gertrude Stein's masterpiece into print for the first time.

the

transatlantic

VOL. II. No. 2
August 1924

Edited in Paris by F. M. FORD

review

CONTENTS

LONDON :
DUCKWORTH & Co., 3 Henrietta St., W.C.2.
2/

NEW YORK :
Thomas Seltzer, Inc.
50 c.

PARIS :
Transatlantic Review Co.
7 FRS. 50

That, twenty years later, was to be the marching song of Hemingway's irregulars when they assisted in, or anticipated, the liberation of Paris. The Paris Hemingway had in mind was the city of idyll and happy marriage and artistic integrity and optimistic youth, never to be recovered. It was a *libération nostalgique.*

For now, it was hard work and little money: he even became a sparring partner again. He was shadow-boxing one day in Ezra

Pound's studio, feinting at a big Chinese vase, when Ford Madox Ford first met him. Ford was conceivably the greatest British novelist of his generation. He wrote too much, as all professional authors must unless they are broken-through and idolized Hemingways. Most of his work is out of print and forgettable (except for the poetry, which is of a high standard), but *The Good Soldier* and *Parade's End* are acknowledged masterpieces. He was also one of the great editors of his time, or of all time, and he was just starting a new magazine in Paris, the *transatlantic review* (this eschewing of upper-case initials was modish). Pound said to Ford, with typical generosity and indiscretion, that Hemingway was the finest prose stylist in the world, and so he must be a natural editorial assistant to a prose stylist less fine, though fine. Hemingway helped Ford, for no pay. His stay with the *transatlantic*, which ended in acrimony, is notable for one considerable achievement – his success in arranging for the serialization of Gertrude Stein's *The Making of Americans* – and for the strange quirk of Hemingway's and Joyce's publishing under a common title – *Work in Progress*. This Joyce was to appropriate entirely for the fragmentary pamphlet publications of the emergent *Finnegans Wake* (a holy name not to be divulged till the book was finished). Hemingway and Joyce maintained a lifelong generosity to each other, rare in both men. Joyce was later to say:

He's a good writer, Hemingway. He writes as he is. We like him. He's a big, powerful peasant, as strong as a buffalo. A sportsman. And ready to live the life he writes about. He would never have written it if his body had not allowed him to live it. But giants of his sort are truly modest; there is much more behind Hemingway's form than people know.

Of Joyce Hemingway said, at the time of his first trip to Africa:*

He was afraid of some things – lightning and things, but a wonderful man. He was under great discipline – his wife, his work, and his bad eyes. His wife was there and she said, yes, his work was too suburban – 'Jim could do with a bit of that lion-hunting.' We would go out to drink and Joyce would fall into a fight. He couldn't even see the man so he'd say: 'Deal with him, Hemingway! Deal with him!'

This amicability is worth noting, since at the time of his work for the *transatlantic review* Hemingway was disclosing very unamiable traits. His moodiness and irascibility were understandable enough in a time of indigent struggle, but a woman friend of Hadley's was sharply noting something more fundamentally dangerous: a capacity for turning against those who helped him, spite, selfishness, viciousness, cruelty. This acute observer was Kitty Cannell, girl friend of Harold Loeb, an expatriate Jew whose main claim to distinction was that he had been the middle-weight boxing champion of Princeton. Loeb loved Hemingway and Hemingway seemed to love Loeb, but Kitty

* See page 65

Ezra Pound, poet, editor, friend of the literary deserving poor, in his Paris studio. Few of those Pound helped, said Hemingway, 'refrained from knifing him at the first opportunity'.

Maxwell Perkins (*opposite above*), Hemingway's editor, at the beginning of his career at Scribners – a few years after the building of the house's headquarters in New York (*right*).

Cannell gave warning of a treachery soon to be fulfilled. She also warned Hadley, whom she considered to be a put-upon and long-suffering angel, that her husband was unreliable. Her prophecies were soundly based, and they were realized in literature as well as life.

In 1925 Hemingway broke through. Edmund Wilson had shown his fellow-Princetonian Scott Fitzgerald the stories and sketches of Hemingway's two Paris volumes, and Fitzgerald, much impressed, had recommended to Maxwell Perkins at Scribners publishing house in New York that he write to Hemingway. Max Perkins was the great publisher's editor, a man who could not write a novel himself but could help real novelists to shape and file their work and make it publishable. He is best known for what he did for Thomas Wolfe, the North Carolina genius who could write a million pulsating words without difficulty but could not bring them to any kind of order. Perkins established a precedent in America that England has been comparatively slow to follow: that the novelist's job is to deliver a load of words to the publisher and then bow to the plastic expertise of the editor. The precedent is, I think, a bad one, though it has been responsible in our own day for highly regarded novels like Joseph Heller's *Catch 22*, which the mavin editor Robert Gottlieb helped to hammer and shape and reduce and polish to the near-masterpiece we have. The invitation to be editorially re-made is one that certain novelists, including myself, continue to resist. Hemingway's sure sense of form and hard-won economy of style rendered him, on the whole, uneditable.

As often happens, Hemingway was receiving attention from two publishers at the same time after a long period of receiving attention from none. Sherwood Anderson's publishers, Boni and Liveright, offered a two-hundred-dollar advance for the volume of stories that Hemingway had now put together under the title of *In Our Time*. Hemingway accepted with joy. Perkins's letter, mailed at the same time as that offer, unaccountably arrived in Paris ten days late. Scribners was the more reputable publisher, but Hemingway was committed to offering a second and third book to Boni and Liveright. His device for getting out of the contract was, to say the least, pusillanimous. He wrote a parody of Sherwood Anderson which, after Turgeniev, he called *The Torrents of Spring*. Anderson's own publishers naturally had to reject it, and he was free to give it, as he was to give all else that he subsequently wrote, to Scribners.

In Our Time is a sizable volume of sixteen stories interleaved with the vignettes that had already appeared in (and I may say now that Hemingway loathed the coy lower case but let Bird have his own way with it) *in our time*. Nick Adams, one of Hemingway's personae, appears in such tales based on boyhood reminiscence as 'Indian Camp' and 'Big Two-Hearted River' – fine stories that help to confirm where Hemingway's talent lay, or lies. He rarely set out deliberately to compose a full-length novel. His way was to start with a short story and, if it showed signs of wishing to expand, to let it have its head. He was essentially perhaps a miniaturist. The vignettes drew on observation more recent than that of the Michigan woods:

Minarets stuck up in the rain out of Adrianople across the mud flats. The carts were jammed for thirty miles along the Karagatch road. Water buffalo and cattle were hauling carts through the mud. No end and no beginning. Just carts loaded with everything they owned. The old men and women, soaked through, walked along keeping the cattle moving. The Maritza was running yellow almost up to the bridge. . . . There was a woman having a kid with a young girl holding a blanket over her and crying. Scared sick looking at it. It rained all through the evacuation.

This is very much the Hemingway style – stark, objective, 'unliterary'. It was a new music and was recognized as such. The critics responded, but the general public did not, not yet. As for *The Torrents of Spring*, it

THE TORRENTS OF SPRING

A ROMANTIC NOVEL IN HONOR OF THE PASSING OF A GREAT RACE

ERNEST HEMINGWAY
AUTHOR OF "IN OUR TIME"

The title-page of Hemingway's pusillanimous satire on Sherwood Anderson.

The Murphys – Gerald and Sara, 'beautiful people' of the twenties whose studio in Paris became Hemingway's home while working on *Men Without Women*. Here they are seen with Hadley and the novelist John Dos Passos at Schruns in Austria, the winter of 1925.

is pure Hemingway in the ineptness of its parody. Sherwood Anderson said a genuine parodist, like Max Beerbohm, could have said it all in a page or two. He, the kindest of men, was too kind. The general view of the time anticipated that of posterity. The only author Hemingway ever proved capable of parodying was himself.

Hemingway was now gathering about him, in Paris, in the Austrian Alps, in Pamplona, the friends who were to be made immortal in *The Sun Also Rises*. This novel, a very great success commercially and a landmark in modern fiction, is called *Fiesta* in England as in most foreign countries. It is a great nuisance to have the same book subsisting in the same language under two different titles, like a man travelling abroad under an alias. But the book is the book,

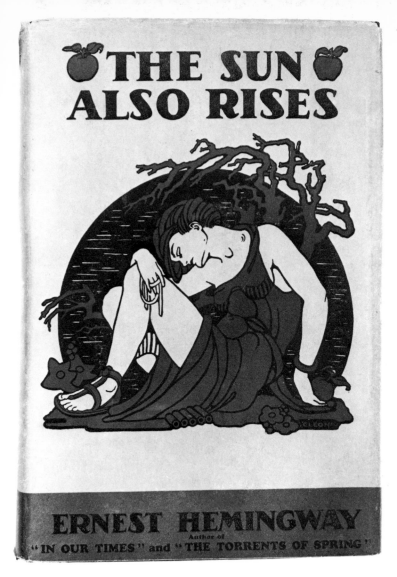

THE SUN ALSO RISES

ERNEST HEMINGWAY
Author of
"IN OUR TIMES" and "THE TORRENTS OF SPRING"

Dust jacket of the first American edition of the novel known in most places as *Fiesta*. The accolades Hemingway received from the Murphys when he read them passages from the novel seemed to confirm that nothing was so fine as the 'fiesta concept of life'.

and in it, hardly disguised, are to be found such personages as Harold Loeb and Lady Duff Twysden, the grey-eyed, cropped-blonde, hard-drinking, hard-loving embodiment of degenerate chic and glamour. Loeb fell heavily for her; Ernest was probably more interested than he appeared to be. But something bigger than mere infidelity to his wife was being prepared for him by the delectably petite Pauline Pfeiffer, who had been a fashion editor for *Vogue* and looked like one of her own models.

There was another friend, well able to contrive his own immortality, and that was Scott Fitzgerald, an author of great skill and delicacy, laureate of the Jazz Age which he baptized if he did not actually invent, with the achievement already behind him of *The Great*

Right: The Murphys and the Hemingways together at Pamplona, 1926. In the middle is Pauline Pfeiffer – the 'unmarried young woman [who] unknowingly, innocently and unrelentingly sets out to marry the husband'. *Below*, on matters mainly literary, Scott Fitzgerald (*right*) had written about Hemingway to Maxwell Perkins in 1924: 'He's the real thing.' On matters partly personal, Hemingway had divined that Zelda Fitzgerald (*left*) was jealous of her husband and obstructive of his talent.

Gatsby, which some have termed the only perfect American novel. Both he and his wife Zelda were wild, spendthrift, and drank heavily. They were outrageous but never coarse, raffish but ever elegant. They were already storing up the materials of their later tragic and spectacular downfalls. Hemingway did not at all take to Zelda, who seemed to him hard and predatory and (which she was) jealous of her husband's talent. Fitzgerald, responsible enough to his art, was irresponsible in nearly everything else. There was, for instance, the occasion when Morley Callaghan, whom Hemingway had known on the *Toronto Star*, and who was to make his name as Canada's finest fiction-writer, visited Paris and boxed with Hemingway. Though four inches shorter, lighter, and out of condition, Callaghan held his own well with the six-foot heavyweight. Fitzgerald kept time. Hemingway lunged at Callaghan, Callaghan got him square on the jaw and felled him. Then Fitzgerald said: 'Oh my God, I let the round go four minutes.' He never forgave his remissness, and, of course, he was not alone in that.

The Sun Also Rises was created mainly out of the events of the Pamplona fiesta of 1925, when Hemingway and Hadley were there with Lady Duff, Harold Loeb, Pat Guthrie (a tall thirsty Scot who was a friend rather than lover of her ladyship), Bill Smith (Hemingway's old friend from Oak Park days). Hemingway pontificated about the bullfighter's art over wine, but, during one of the amateur sessions, Loeb seized the horns of one of the bulls and did an acrobatic ride across the arena. This made Hemingway jealous. Moreover, he developed a possessive attitude towards Lady Duff which manifested itself not in a desire to make love to her – though she was evidently willing enough – but in a strong resentment of Loeb's apparent success with her earlier that summer. There was a dog-in-the-manger attitude which must have had something to do with the coming rejection of Hadley. The amorous field was not exactly wide open for Hemingway, but he was a sort of guardian of the gate. What seems to have driven him into the writing of this first novel was a tangle of emotions that had to be cathartized, in which guilt, animus and velleity jostled. So Harold Loeb becomes Robert Cohn, the hero's 'tennis friend', a character perhaps intended to be detestable but – since art is more compassionate than people – in fact merely, and touchingly, comic. Lady Duff becomes Lady Brett. Hemingway becomes Jake Barnes (in the first drafts Hem or Ernie), a journalist with a war wound that makes him physically incapable of love, hopelessly in love with Brett. The vicarious assumption of impotence is interesting; the war wound dramatizes a sexual diffidence or psychological block that is the other side of the coin of the tough hirsute man of action.

People and places out of which *The Sun Also Rises* was created. *Opposite: Above*, Pamplona, 1925. Hemingway may be seen at the right, in the path of the angry bull. *Below*, Charles Hopkins, Hemingway, Bill Smith. Hopkins – whom Hemingway called Hoopkins or the Hooper – had been a colleague on the *Kansas City Star*. Smith was from St Louis, a friend from the Oak Park days. *Left: Above*, Hemingway, Hadley and others enjoy themselves, Pamplona, 1925. *Below*, Hemingway, a few years later, demonstrates the brotherhood of bull and man.

Hemingway and Pauline, the second Mrs Hemingway.

Sara and Gerald Murphy (the figures to the right) in the Vienna of the 1920s.

Hemingway's personages pursue an empty alcoholic life in Paris, then, at Pamplona, are involved in the regenerative cleansing ritual of the bullfight. There is something of Eliot's *The Waste Land* in the book, though Hemingway – who read it when it first appeared in 1922 – never professed any admiration or even understanding of the poem. Jake is a kind of Fisher King, aware of the aridity of life without love but stricken, cut off from the enactment of desire like any Prufrock. Salvation depends on sacrifice – not that of the Mass (Jake is Catholic, as Hemingway – allegedly converted in Italy – nominally was), but of a ritual in which real blood flows. Enough blood flowed in the war, but the conflict of man and bull elects the confrontation with death and, in a sense, controls death. All this, of course, is grossly to oversimplify.

The novel stands as a record of a 'lost generation'. The phrase came from Gertrude Stein, or rather the proprietor of the garage to which she took her car for repair: he said there were no good mechanics among the young men back from the war: they were a *génération perdue*. The title comes from Ecclesiastes, and the religious resonances, though damped, give extra meaning to flat slangy statements like 'I feel like hell'. It is not a depressing book, rather the opposite: it celebrates the abiding earth and the life of the body – the running stream, the sun on the back of the neck, the wine that is also blood, the coming to terms with death, food. Jake makes a heavy meal at the end; though impotent he is able to 'like a lot of things'. *The Sun Also Rises* is, in the worn term, 'life-enhancing'. When it came out in October 1926 it excited not only the critics but the general public. It was one of the rare books able to influence the way people behaved and talked. Brett became a model of speech and behaviour for a whole generation of college girls. The Hemingway male – tough, battered, stoic, laconic, making a style out of despair – began to appear in the better-class bars. Hemingway, not yet thirty, had arrived.

Everything has to be paid for. The days of obscurity and penurious struggle were coming to an end, so were the days of idyllic innocence, trust, fidelity, integrity. Pauline Pfeiffer told Ernest that she loved him; Ernest reciprocated. Hadley wondered how genuine was his desire for a divorce. If, she said, he and Pauline would agree to a hundred-day separation and, at the end, found themselves still in love, then they could go ahead and marry. So Pauline returned to the United States, and Ernest lived a bachelor existence in Paris, working hard at a volume of stories in a studio on the rue Froidevaux on the Left Bank. This studio belonged to Gerald Murphy, a wealthy graduate of Yale. He and his wife Sara were known as the happiest couple in the world, as well as the most charming and hospitable. They are, to some extent, the models for the protagonists of Scott Fitzgerald's *Tender is the Night*.

Happy times for Hadley and Bumby in Paris, 1924. Hemingway strongly expressed his sense of guilt at destroying the marriage.

They did not write, but they knew all the writers. Hemingway, riddled with guilt and remorse, tortured by nightmares, wept like a child when Hadley ordered the division of their furniture. There was also the matter of Bumby, not easily divisible. He loved his father far above French grammar: *La vie est beau avec papa*, he would say. Hemingway arranged to have all the royalties from the American and British editions of *The Sun Also Rises* paid to Hadley, the least he could do. Hadley said he could have his divorce right away. Ernest said he was a son of a bitch; others – especially the originals of *The Sun Also Rises* – said the same. Oak Park was censorious about the book. Ernest's mother wrote sweetly that she believed he would still do something worthwhile if he trusted in God and tried to love Him. Ernest kept on saying that he was a son of a bitch.

The title of the new collection of stories was to be *Men Without Women* – tough tales of tough characters untempered by the gentler sex. Hemingway, between marriages, was not easy to get on with. He was seeing much of Archibald MacLeish, the poet, and his wife Ada. Ada deplored Ernest's truculence in public and noted that he always picked on little men. When, at last, Ernest and Pauline had their Catholic wedding at Passy, Ada was nauseated at the easy way in which he affirmed that this was his one true marriage, Pauline being a good St Louis Catholic and himself a convert under fire. As for Hadley, she was a St Louis Protestant; their marriage had never been valid. So much for the years of trust and love, the worse not the better, the poorer not the richer.

Key West, Florida, where
Hemingway found the sea full of
exciting quarry. His parents meet
Pauline.

Life, if not literature, did its best to punish him. His book of stories
was published in 1927 and did well, but he developed a bad attack of
grippe, as well as toothache and haemorrhoids, compounded with
virtual blindness when Bumby, permitted to be with him for a time,
dug his fingernail into his father's one good eye. He went skiing with
MacLeish and suffered ten bad spills. Back in Paris the skylight in the
bathroom fell on him, gouging his head and necessitating nine stitches.
He had started a new novel and wondered whether he wanted to finish
it in Paris. Things had turned sour. It had been bliss but was bliss no
longer. He summed it all up many years later in *A Moveable Feast*:

Before these rich had come we had already been infiltrated by another rich
using the oldest trick there is. It is that an unmarried young woman becomes
the temporary best friend of another young woman who is married, goes to
live with the husband and wife and then unknowingly, innocently and
unrelentingly sets out to marry the husband. . . . The husband has two
attractive girls around him when he has finished work. One is new and
strange and if he has bad luck he gets to love them both. . . .

When I saw my wife again standing by the tracks as the train came in by
the piled logs at the station, I wished I had died before I ever loved anyone but
her. She was smiling, the sun on her lovely face tanned by the snow and sun,
beautifully built, her hair red-gold in the sun, grown out all winter
awkwardly and beautifully, and Mr Bumby standing with her, blond and
chunky and with winter cheeks. . . .

I loved her and I loved no one else and we had a lovely magic time when we were alone. I worked well and we made great trips, and I thought we were invulnerable again. . . . That was the end of the first part of Paris. Paris was never to be the same again. . . .

He became homesick for America, not just for one place – like Oak Park, to which he had no desire to go back – but for its vague great green spaces and beasts and rivers. The homesickness came at the right time: Pauline was pregnant and, like Hadley before her, needed to have her child on home soil. Before, it had been Canada, now it was to be the opposite end of the continent. John Dos Passos sent them there, raving about the beauty of the Florida keys, especially Key West. Key West became the mature Hemingway's first American home.

In Paris he had reticently professed a devotion to art unmatched among the café aesthetes, but his pose had been that of a tough and sweaty philistine. In Key West his aim was not to stand out as a Great Writer among the sailors and fisherfolk but to appear to be a mysterious and dangerous man from the north – big bootlegger or head of dope ring. Muscular, hulking, with the skylight scar on his brow, profane of speech, he was delighted to be taken for anything but a writer. This superficial disavowal of a high vocation is frequently to be found among Anglo-Saxon artists, though rarely among French. Sir Edward Elgar, at the height of his power and fame, even appeared to be ashamed of having written great music: he posed as a hippic man, defiantly at the races while *The Dream of Gerontius* was being performed in the Queen's Hall. Hemingway's books were to buy him the leisure to be a fulltime man of action, converting his entire maturity to a kind of blown-up childhood summer in the Michigan woods. But in Key West he found something bigger than those woods: the wide deep sea, crammed with tarpon, red snapper, amberjack and barracuda. He became a passionate fisherman.

The time for permanently settling by the sea was not yet. Hemingway had to meet his new mother-in-law in Piggott, Arkansas, and then take Pauline to have her baby on what was a sort of home ground – Kansas City. They stayed with Malcolm Lowry and his wife on Indian Lake until her labour pains began. He himself was in intense labour with the novel that was to be called *A Farewell to Arms*. Lowry was, over ten years later, to produce after immense effort *Under the Volcano*, a remarkable novel that continues, after numerous promotions and repromotions, to fail to catch on with the general public. Hemingway was luckier than he knew. What with him was an aesthetic revolution seemed to that general public to be a kind of boy's-book simplicity. The public swallowed his complexities like oysters. The complexities of *Under the Volcano* proclaimed themselves in

Hemingway and Bumby at Key West, 1928. The start of ambitious fishing.

Hemingway and his father demonstrating friendship, in spite of the son's feeling 'so much older than his father . . . that he could hardly bear it'.

a style that required much masticating. But superficially Hemingway and Lowry had much in common – hard-drinking men, exiles, self-punishing, tragedy brewing in them unsuspected.

Pauline's labour was excruciating. A boy, to be christened Patrick, was delivered by Caesarean section in 1928 while Hemingway was dispassionately writing about the death in childbirth of his heroine. As for fatherhood, he had lost the capacity to find it exhilarating; indeed, a more general disenchantment with life – the kind cruelly associated with success – was manifesting itself. The successful writer can live where he wants to live, and where he wants to live is anywhere except where he has decided to live. Fishing and hunting in Wyoming, he was homesick for Paris. But, he knew, in Paris he would be hungry for Key West. And, wherever he was except Spain, he knew there was no place like Spain. Dissatisfaction was temporarily exploded by shock, shame, and the fatigue of a new responsibility – that of head of the Hemingway family – when he learned that his father had shot himself. Ed Hemingway had been worrying about the state of his finances but even more about his physical condition. Unable to sleep because of diabetes and angina pectoris, he had put a Civil War pistol to his right ear and made an end of things. Hemingway was against suicide not only as a nominal Catholic but because it violated his code of courage.

Death was certain but life was good. The courting of death was an aspect of the good life, but the embracing of death was forbidden. Grace must always be maintained under pressure, no matter how killing the pressure. He was bitterly ashamed of what his father had done.

A Farewell to Arms came out to rave reviews and handsome sales when he was back in irresistible Paris. He had taken the title from the *Oxford Book of English Verse*, as later he was to take *For Whom the Bell Tolls* from the *Oxford Book of English Prose*. His titles and epigraphs did

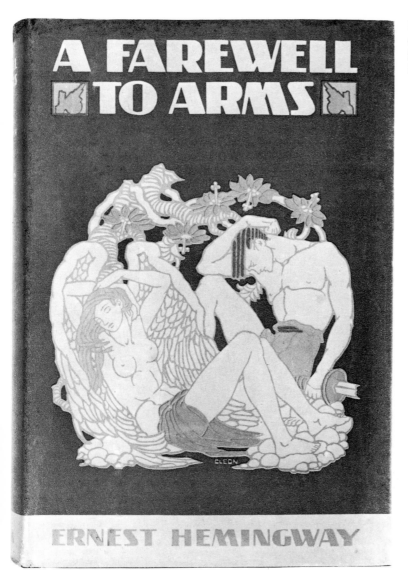

Dust jacket of the first American edition of 'my long tale of transalpine fornication including the entire war in Italy and so to BED'. 1929.

In the late summer of that year
we lived in a house in a village that —

~~In the night we heard the troops~~

looked across the river and the plain to the
mountains. ~~The river ran in~~ clear channels in the
boulders and the river bed was white pebbles and dry white
~~The water in the river~~
bed of white pebbles the water was clear and swiftly moving and blue in the
and white boulders and
Troops went by the house
~~This river along~~
and down the ~~road~~ road and the dust
they raised powdered the leaves of the trees.
The trunks of the trees too were dusty and the
leaves fell early that year and we saw
~~seen~~ the troops marching along the road and
the dust rising and leaves stirred by the breeze
falling and
the soldiers marching and afterwards the
road bare and white except for the leaves.

not emerge out of profound reading but from superficial though prolonged search for what sounded good. *A Farewell to Arms* is the name of a poem by Shakespeare's contemporary George Peele. The poem itself has no relevance to the novel:

> *His golden locks Time hath to silver turn'd;*
> *O Time too swift, O swiftness never ceasing;*
> *His youth 'gainst time and age hath ever spurn'd,*
> *But spurn'd in vain; youth waneth by increasing:*
> *Beauty, strength, youth, are flowers but fading seen;*
> *Duty, faith, love, are roots, and ever green.*

And yet Hemingway's authority is such that his title no longer seems to be a theft. In late 1929, after serialization in *Scribner's Magazine*, the appearance of the novel inspired a popular song called, predictably, *Farewell to Arms*:

> *Farewell to arms*
> *That softly caressed me –*
> *Farewell to arms,*
> *Good-bye to love. . . .*

George Peele had been left far behind.

Ten years after the end of the First World War, the war novels were beginning to appear – *Her Privates We*, by 'Private 19022' (Frederic Manning), *All Quiet on the Western Front*, by Erich Maria von Remarque, *Death of a Hero*, by Richard Aldington – as well as such war memoirs as Robert Graves's *Goodbye to All That* (another popular song came out of this: 'I used to dream, I used to scheme – goodbye to all that . . .'). The long gestation had been as necessary for *A Farewell to Arms* as for the others, but Hemingway had to purge his system not only of the war on the Italian front but his unconsummated passion for Agnes von Kurowsky. Agnes is transformed into the British nurse Catherine Barkley, and she returns the love of Frederic Henry, a Hemingway who has actually fought and even experienced the retreat from Caporetto. She dies in childbirth, thus stressing one of the main themes of the book, the unity of life and death (retreating soldiers, cartridge boxes under their capes, march 'as though they were six months gone with child'). We have, on the surface, a highly romantic love story which ends as all such stories must – with the death of one of the lovers – but we have also, in very fine prose, a complex statement about the nature of human commitment, presented against a background of war vividly caught. With this novel Hemingway got the best of both worlds: he achieved a complex artistry perhaps greater than that of *The Sun Also Rises*; he became a highly popular writer.

Indeed, it was only three years after the publication of the book that he began to reach a public not at all given to reading but very ready for

Opposite: Opening of the first draft of *A Farewell to Arms*. The revisions, in pencil and later on the typewriter, were extensive.

a more direct romantic fiction. *A Farewell to Arms* had its first filming in 1932, with Gary Cooper as Frederic, Helen Hayes as Catherine, and Adolphe Menjou as the Italian captain Rinaldi. This deferred to popular taste by ending the story with a living Catherine, to Hemingway's disgust, and it began a whole unsatisfactory saga of bad Hemingway movies. In 1958 there was a more skilful and less compromising adaptation of *A Farewell to Arms,* with Rock Hudson, Jennifer Jones and Vittorio de Sica (directed by Charles Vidor), but it could not match in visual language the distinction of the Hemingway prose. No better proof is needed of the essentially 'literary' nature of Hemingway's work than a long succession of cinematic mediocrities based on his work. What, at a superficial reading, seems to be a bare scenario with crisp film dialogue turns out to be a highly wrought verbal artefact in which meaning resides wholly in the rhythms of the language. *The Killers* is the only Hemingway film of distinction, and it was the only one that Hemingway would watch: he was to do this regularly in Cuba on his home projector, though he usually fell asleep during the second reel.

Hemingway was now thirty, and the world's grim 'thirties were beginning, their cacophonic prelude the Wall Street crash (he worried about the effect this might have on his sales, but he was always to be from now on a bestseller). He had used up much of his past in novels and stories and was henceforth to stay with the present. The 'twenties had been a remarkable decade in all the arts, and one city above all others had seemed to nourish it: the Paris from which the Americans were now going home had been the Mecca of various and brilliant creation. Even the wealthy dilettantes and the pretentious failures had lent flavour to the time and place. What would Paris have been without men like Harry Crosby – founder of the Black Sun Press, seducer, drunk, bad poet, sensational New York suicide of 1929 – or the nameless writers and painters who talked like geniuses and excreted polychrome trash? Paris had no magic to give talent to the talentless: she had merely provided an ambience in which art was taken seriously, a tradition of sodality among artists, and – not least – a fair number of francs to the dollar. Paris had presided over the Modern Movement, which expressed itself as a rejection of the doctrine of Liberal Man – man progressing, mastering his environment, finding salvation in science and the rational organization of society. European liberal optimism had foundered in the war. The human instincts were now to be more important than the reason: Natural or Animal or Unconscious Man replaced the H. G. Wells *Uebermensch* and the open conspiracy of the planning intellect. The men who came out of the war were weary, but only of worn shibboleths; they had energy enough to build new art based on rejection of the pre-war heritage. Everything had to be re-made – the language of literature, the sonorities of music, the phenomenography of the visual arts. In literature, James Joyce – a chronic exile, no mere expatriate – was to stay on in Paris till it fell in 1940 and push modernity to the limit. *Finnegans Wake* was published in 1939 and forms a fitting conclusion to the age of *l'entre deux guerres*. But Hemingway, who found his idiom in Paris and was now satisfied with it, was destined for success in an environment where it could only mean a sort of moral, or aesthetic, corruption. He wrote fine things after *A Farewell to Arms*, but he did not, like Joyce, wish to break new ground.

Hemingway had arrived; he saw himself as one of the patriarchs of American literature, young as he was. He began to be everyone's papa, but not often a benevolent one. He specialized in pontifical assertions, high-handed rebukes, brutal threats, double-fisted punishments. He loftily told Scott Fitzgerald how to write his own novels. He met Allen Tate – the distinguished Southern poet and critic who, perhaps reluctantly, had to admit that *A Farewell to Arms* was a masterpiece – and told him that the number of orgasms decreed for a man was fixed at birth, and that a man should not make love too much in his youth, reserving some of those orgasms for middle age. (Another oblique admission of sexual insufficiency in himself?) He also said, without evidence, that Ford Madox Ford was sexually impotent. He discovered that Archibald MacLeish, unable to support a family on his poetry, had taken a job with Henry Luce's magazine *Fortune*, and he laid down the law about artistic integrity, boasting that he himself (to whom Luce had just offered $1,000 for 2,500 words about bullfighting) was above such mean compromise. The journal *Bookman* had attacked Hemingway as a 'dirty' writer, and Hemingway offered to go over there and beat hell out of the editor. His old friend and publisher, McAlmon, was, according to Scott Fitzgerald, telling people that Pauline was lesbian and Ernest a fag and a wife-beater. Hemingway said that McAlmon was too pitiable to be beaten to a pulp, but that he supposed he ought to get over there and break his bones for his own good. Morley Callaghan was said to be saying that he had administered the KO to Hemingway, and Hemingway sent a raging cable demanding a public apology. Hemingway was creating a tough-guy persona, that of a poor kid who'd had to battle his way to the top and, with a few books behind him, was already a scarred literary veteran well qualified to deliver sound advice to the literary tyro (Scott Fitzgerald, for example). The uncharitable might say that Hemingway the bully and liar was now in full flower; the more uncharitable that all this was nothing compared with what was to come; the least uncharitable that he was one hell of a fine writer and was entitled to his fibs and tantrums.

A generic portrait of Hemingway in the 1920s – tough, handsome, distrustful.

Nature, as usual, administered her chastisements. She even told him not to overeat and overdrink – which he, the arrived and famous, felt entitled to do – by swelling his fingers into sausages after a season of gorging in Spain. Hemingway was to be a gross enough eater for one who had spent his early creative years in the land of the *haute cuisine*, a man with a taste for Bermuda onions and red wine for breakfast, with dollops of chutney and mustard pickle on his morning meat, marmalade on rank bearsteaks. He became a very formidable drinker. The manager of the Gritti Palace in Venice tells me that three bottles of Valpolicella first thing in the day were nothing to him, and then there were the daiquiris, Scotch, tequila, bourbon, vermouthless martinis. The physical punishment he took from alcohol was delayed and was, in a sense, actively courted; the other punishments were gratuitous, it seemed, and very immediate – kidney trouble from fishing in chill Spanish waters, a torn groin muscle from something unspecified when he was visiting Palencia, a finger gashed to the bone in a mishap with a punchbag, the laceration of arms and legs and face

from thorns and branches when carried through a deep Wyoming wood on a runaway horse. And much more to come.

Key West now became home. It was a hot and humid island cooled by the Atlantic trades, with low sailors' bars, Spanish restaurants, coconut palms, and old white houses of a certain rundown elegance. It was ancient pirate territory, but the waters were full now of legitimate traffic. There was a bar synonymous with the better known one in Havana (only a hundred miles away) – Sloppy Joe's. Carmen Miranda was to celebrate that in a song; Bing Crosby was to croon 'See you in C.U.B.A.'. Cuba was an American playground in those days; soon it was to seem more *simpatico* to Hemingway, more *echt*, than Key West. But in the meantime Key West, and the old stone house Pauline's uncle gave them as a belated wedding present, was a good place to come back to after tarpon-fishing in the Tortugas waters or bear-hunting in Wyoming.

Hemingway would now have been getting along nicely with his writing had it not been for a car accident in Wyoming. Blinded by

Hemingway's house at Key West, Florida. Key West was maritime, tropical, relaxed, a bit decrepit, hot and saltily humid. Sailors fought in bars full of rumba music. The place suited Hemingway.

Maxwell Perkins, greatest of publishers' editors, with Hemingway at Key West, Florida, in January 1935.

oncoming headlights, he swerved his Ford into a ditch, where it lay on top of him. His arm was complicatedly broken. He was able to tell Max Perkins that, since signing on with Scribners, he had had anthrax infection, a cut eyeball, a huge glass-gash in his forehead, kidney trouble, a sliced finger, a torn face and leg and arm, and now a fracture of the instrument with which he earned a living. Naturally, he also talked of going to Africa, where, he said, you must pull the trigger only when you are close enough to smell the lion's halitosis.

The book he was trying to write about this time was *Death in the Afternoon*, a lengthy study of the metaphysics of bullfighting published in 1932. It entailed frequent trips to Spain, where a revolution was proceeding, though it was not permitted to get in the way of the *corridas*. The clergy Hemingway met *en voyage* – Spanish priests exiled from Mexico, where they had had their own revolution – feared that the republican mobs would be ravishing nuns and burning churches. But Madrid, though one hundred per cent republican, seemed orderly if noisy. As a nominal Catholic, Hemingway should have been on the side of the Carlists, who made Pamplona roar with the shout of *Viva Cristo Rey*, but his nominalism did not prevent his being – quite unpolitically – on the side of the people, long tyrannized, now exulting in what was to prove a very transitory freedom. As for true Catholics and Anglo-Catholics of liberal persuasion, it was a very awkward time. The Spanish Church had never been separate from gross secular inequality and governmental corruption; one had to hate priests and bishops along with the deposed monarchy. Some Anglo-Saxon Catholics, like the South African poet Roy Campbell, were to be logical in fighting for Franco when the time came. Others, like Evelyn Waugh, were to exhibit a prudent reticence during the conflict. Hemingway was to support the Spanish people without active belligerence, the Remington typewriter being more potent than the Remington gun; his Catholicism, being nominal, could be temporarily or even permanently suspended without overmuch spiritual anxiety. He was to be clear-eyed about the whole Spanish situation, seeing in the brief republican heaven little more than a proliferation of bureaucracy and not much amelioration of the lot of the common people. In the meantime, the cult of the bull ran deeper than politics.

Death in the Afternoon appeared in 1932. It is a curious production, sometimes tedious, sometimes of absorbing interest. The Hemingway of the early reportage for the *Toronto Star* was a man who saw things sharply and sharply delivered what he saw, keeping himself discreetly in the background. When it was necessary for him to come forward and make a judgment, it was usually done with a flash of individuality wholly charming. The Hemingway of the bull book is always there, papa, big daddy, all-knowing, bullying, sometimes a bore, often very self-indulgent, always self-aware. Max Eastman's title for the review he wrote was 'Bull in the Afternoon', apt enough. He chastised Hemingway, justly enough, for the false tough stance and the romantic gush and the tendency, inseparable from toughness, to sentimentalize.

For all that, there is in *Death in the Afternoon* a good deal of solid information about the bullfighter's art, as well as the author's somewhat rambling disquisitions on the nature of life and death. He claims to know the Spanish, and especially the Castilian, attitude to these two bedfellows – the endless dark or nothingness or *nada* following the brief shaft of sun. In a short story, a masterly one called 'A Clean Well-Lighted Place', he presents very vividly this avoidance of *nada* in the image of the waiter who rejoices in the clean well-lighted restaurant where he works and does not want to go out into the dark. Here he gives us more than images; he gives us wordy philosophy. Life is too short for anything but the one thing that can outface death – human dignity. But it may be possible also to get the better of death by reducing it to a servant, making it do its work at our call, learning the art of killing so that death can be sung as a song is sung. This killing must not be battlefield or abattoir slaughter. The bull is chosen as a

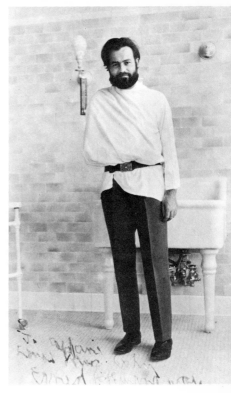

Hemingway in hospital in Billings, Montana, after his Wyoming car accident, November 1930 – an episode out of which the humorous short story, 'The Gambler, the Nun, and the Radio' evidently developed. The photograph was signed for his bibliographer, Louis Cohn, with his left hand.

ERNEST HEMINGWAY

DEATH IN THE AFTER-NOON

CHARLES SCRIBNERS SONS

Dust jacket of the first American edition. The Castilians, it is said in the book, 'know death is the unescapable reality, the one thing any man may be sure of'. Max Eastman's critical review was an accurate indication that Hemingway the poseur was making his appearance.

victim because he is big and strong and endowed with free will like all of God's higher creation. There is even a divinity in him which goes back to Mithraism. He can choose to kill, and the matador deliberately courts the possibility of his own death as a gesture of human pride and dignity and panache. Triumph and tragedy are linked in the ritual, which is rooted in ancient pagan doctrines of human courage and virtue.

Hemingway goes too far sometimes. He does not seem to see that, to the majority of those crowding the arena, bullfighting is satisfying because of the certainty of grave injury and often death, that the spectators are baying for blood as ignobly as any Roman mob goggle-eyed at Christians torn by starving lions. When the picador's horse has his guts ripped out, that is, Hemingway says, a mere comic interlude in the purple tragedy proceeding to the moment of truth. He anthropomorphizes the brave bull into a stiff-upper-lip hero that scorns to groan or bellow. Hemingway is making the *corrida* exteriorize certain movements of his own soul. The obsession with death and killing seems to spring out of guilt, and we divine that he has not got over his abandonment of a loved wife. There is a certain hysteria, expressed in uncharacteristic loose and repetitive writing, as well as in a gratuitous parade of Goya-like images of destruction. He appears to want to make the reader feel unclean and uncomfortable because that is the way he feels himself.

To anyone who, like myself, has lived on the Iberian peninsula, *Death in the Afternoon* sheds many of its faults as it becomes weathered by time, settling into the condition of a classic. I have never liked bullfighting, and I have never wished to learn to like it, but I find myself unable to ignore the metaphors of its ritual. I have eaten the broiled flesh of a slain bull after a *corrida*, and can testify to a curious sense of sacramental participation as valid as that of the Church to which, less nominally than Hemingway, I have belonged. There is insight and truth in this book, and perhaps the foliage of nonsense, the barroom metaphysics, the pompous longueurs are necessary to set them off. It is not a book easy to shrug away.

Obsessed with death, especially with the deaths of the marlin he had begun gleefully to administer in Cuban waters, Hemingway was not too happy when it seemed to be pointing the finger at himself. Sweating after a vain struggle with a monster fish, he was overtaken by a shower of rain and caught bronchial pneumonia. Convalescing, he corrected the galleys of his new book and saw at the top of each long sheet certain innocent but ominous ciphers: '4 Gal 80.. Hemingway's Death $11\frac{1}{2}$ – 14 Scotch.' Here, of course, was a mere printer's abbreviation of his full title, but it looked as if Hemingway had downed too much whisky and done for himself: four gallons of eighty proof, fourteen doubles – it all fitted in. Superstitious, morbidly touchy, he growled about wringing various bastards' necks, and then he went moodily off to kill elk and moose, black bears and little birds.

Death in the Afternoon, unlike *A Farewell to Arms*, was not celebrated in popular song. It belatedly gave its name to a cocktail, however, which I first met in the airport bar of Auckland, New Zealand: a mixture of absinthe and champagne, not ineptly titled. Hemingway got far from high on the far from laudatory reviews the books received. Eastman said something about Hemingway's literary style being like 'false hair on the chest', and Hemingway exploded. Eastman, he said, was a swine and a traitor and also impotent and jealous as hell of a real man who 'could beat the shit out of any of them' and could write as well. One of these days, he said, he would pound Eastman to a pulp. He eventually got his chance in Max Perkins's office, where he found the other Max conferring with the editor about his new book of essays. Hemingway was content at first to compare, smiling, his haired chest with Eastman's hairless one; then he saw that Eastman proposed including 'Bull in the Afternoon' in the collection of essays and started to beat him up. Nobody was really hurt.

He could not offer to knock hell out of Gertrude Stein, who said nasty things about him in her memoirs, *The Autobiography of Alice B. Toklas* (Miss Toklas was Miss Stein's friend and companion). She stressed how Hemingway derived his style from herself and Sherwood Anderson and said also that this somewhat shameful offspring was 'yellow'. Hemingway retorted that she was 'queer and liked only queers'; as for himself, he was not 'queer', he had *cojones*, he could also write, and there was going to be a great new collection of stories (*Winner Take Nothing*) to prove it, God damn the lot of them. To prove his sexual capacity he began to contribute tough sporting articles to a new magazine for men, one with real chest-hair and genuine *cojones*, though its name was regrettably milk-toast and genteel, to say nothing of limily snobbish: *Esquire*. He would show the bastards.

All this time Pauline remained a good wife and a staunch pal and gave him another son to add to his existing two by two wives. Unfortunately, there was an old superstition about a man who could not beget daughters being somewhat less than a man, but let that pass, there was time enough for daughters. The first wife, Hadley, eased his guilt at his desertion of her by marrying Paul Scott Mowrer, the new editor of the *Chicago Daily News*. The way would be open soon for Hemingway's second desertion, qualified, like the first, by a sort of fidelity, since the third wife too would be a St Louis woman. For the present, Pauline was the right sort of wife to have, for she was very willing to go with him to Africa, there to shoot at wild beasts.

Hemingway had had the costly safari in mind for a year or so. It was not just a matter of curiosity about the dark continent; he had started to develop a philosophy of heroism, and this had to be tested in action. The American frontiers had all been won, the age of Natty Bumppo was over. You could not always have a major war to test grit and trigger-finger. Bullfighting was an activity undoubtedly heroic, but you had to be a bullfighter, and preferably a Spaniard, to engage in it. Hemingway had done his best for bullfighting (he alleged he had seen a thousand bulls killed before writing *Death in the Afternoon*), but he had always been in the stands, never the arena. In Africa he could act directly, not vicariously. True, he had dared the deep waters and

the big fish, but fish were not flesh of one's flesh, like bulls. Lions were, proverbially, even nobler and more dangerous than bulls. So he had to go to Africa to kill some.

Ernest and Pauline landed at Mombasa in the late autumn of 1932, then made the long train-trip to Nairobi. From there they went to Machakos in the Mua Hills, where the great white hunter Philip Percival was soon ready to lead them on safari. The two men took to each other. Percival was courteous, brave, full of fine tales of the chase. Hemingway had to wear spectacles to shoot, but he was quick and eager to learn, also charming, also humble. The humility was naturally to wear away as he developed skill in killing kongoni, impala, guinea fowl and gazelle. The gunbearer, M'Cora or M'Cola, was not impressed by Hemingway, nor indeed by any of the men on the trip, but he thought highly of Pauline, who was about his own size and whom he called *mama*. Pauline was the first to take a pot at a lion, but Ernest, banging with his Springfield immediately after her, felled it while she had merely winged it. M'Cora or M'Cola and the rest of the boys swore it was Pauline's lion: *Mama piga simba.* They sang the lion-song and bore her round the camp on their shoulders. Hemingway did not like this too well: other people should not cheat.

But he got what was undoubtedly his own lion a little later, right in the neck. There was pride in the achievement, but also shame. The flies descended on the copious blood of the beast; the fine kingly creature with its dark mane and muscles still twitching under the tawny hide has been defiled, its wound was an obscene nest of shrilling flies. And he, Hemingway, was responsible for its degradation. He had to be punished, so amoebic dysentery struck. More, he developed a prolapse of the lower intestine. He had to be flown, in pain and with difficulty, to a hospital in Nairobi, there to be injected with emetine. He felt better soon and better still when he learned that his book of stories, *Winner Take Nothing*, was selling well. You always had to take the rough with the smooth.

You had to take the tsetse flies and the snakes and the damned cowardly hyenas (which all had their counterparts in the world of letters), along with the thrill of felling rhino and buffalo (which was like the thrill of finishing a book though more easily bought). And you also had to take the disappointment of not killing as big a kudu as the next man. Still, when the rains came and it was all over, he had to admit that he had done pretty well. He had also, though this lay ahead, got a moderate book out of it and perhaps his two best short stories.

It was the voyage home on the *Ile de France* that blessed Hemingway with a new and glamorous friend. Marlene Dietrich made a stunning descent to the dining saloon one evening to join a dinner party. Counting twelve already there at table, she superstitiously withdrew, but Hemingway, full of charm and quick as a flash, confronted her and said he would gladly make the fourteenth. He was always to admire her and, as a token of affection, call her 'the Kraut'. He never boasted of having taken her to bed, saying that they always fancied each other at the wrong time – when one of them was engaged in another amour. He gave her avuncular advice which she regularly took; he did not kid her as he kidded the other kids; he granted her the unusual privilege of addressing him by his baptismal name. He was, one thinks, a little afraid of her.

The horns and heads and hides and other tangible trophies of the African adventure were to come later by another ship and were to cost dear. But, home in Key West, the unpacking of the bags of experience into a book to be called *Green Hills of Africa* could begin almost at once. It is proper to examine this book briefly now. It is not a good book, but it is meant to be a happy one. If the bullfight book sees death tragically, the lionhunt one looks on the gratuitous killing of beasts lightheartedly, innocently, in terms of a manly sporting code and the hearty healthiness of fair competition. 'I did not mind killing anything ... if I killed it cleanly. . . . They all had to die. . . . And I had no guilty

Marlene Dietrich, a life-long friend of Hemingway, embodiment of Hollywood glamour, nicknamed ungallantly 'the Kraut'.

feelings at all.' The work has the loose structure of a plotless novel, but all the characters are real people, with Hemingway as the hero, rifle butt on foot, whisky flask between knees, 'feeling the cool wind of the night and smelling the good smell of Africa. I was altogether happy.' That he is not altogether happy we can take as read: there is too much crying aloud of how good it all is. The massive simplifications of sport mask a fundamental disquiet, perhaps best personified in the image of the dying hyena, maddened, eating its own guts. The hyena is always the villain, but not even villains ought to suffer too much. Hemingway, from whom intimations of mortality are never far, tries to get the better of death by 'cleanly' administering it, but there has to be something neurotically unsound about this obsession with firing lead at lions and kudu. One can accept a concern with daily death, as we can in *Death in the Afternoon*, if there is a candid acceptance of the absurdity of life, but here it is all Edenic sweetness and the joy of the chase. Perhaps the most embarrassing aspect of the work, as of much of Hemingway's later work, is the endless need to prove virility, not a notable trait of the genuinely virile.

I must be quick to qualify this dim view of Hemingway's African memories with laudation of the two stories that came out in 1936, within a month of each other, in *Esquire*. At the beginning of the year, in that same *cojonado* magazine, Scott Fitzgerald published his remarkable three articles about his now mythical 'crack-up', a prolonged cry of despair which Hemingway was ready to sneer at in private and, in public, magisterially diagnose. The diagnosis appears in 'The Snows of Kilimanjaro', where the dying writer Harry muses on 'poor Scott Fitzgerald' as a man in love with the rich (different from the rest of us. Yes, they have more money), bemused by the glamour of success, learning too late that his 'romantic awe' was misplaced, shuddering at a devastating truth, wrecked by the collapse of a philosophy. But Harry himself, though not given to romantic whining, has followed the wrong gods and wasted his talent. Now he is dying of a gangrened leg on a hot African plain, looking up at the snowcap of Kilimanjaro. Hemingway had learned from the white hunter Percival that, incredibly, the frozen corpse of a leopard had been found up there. In the story the 'clean' death of the overreaching predator and the dirty painless death through gangrene are used as symbols of considerable power. The beast signifies the artist who dies nobly, seeking the summit, and the gangrene stands for the corruption and mortification of the talent misused, prostituted, permitted to atrophy.

In the film of 'The Snows of Kilimanjaro' (1952, directed by Henry King, with Gregory Peck, Susan Hayward and Ava Gardner), the ironical happy ending of Harry's dying vision – the conquest of the

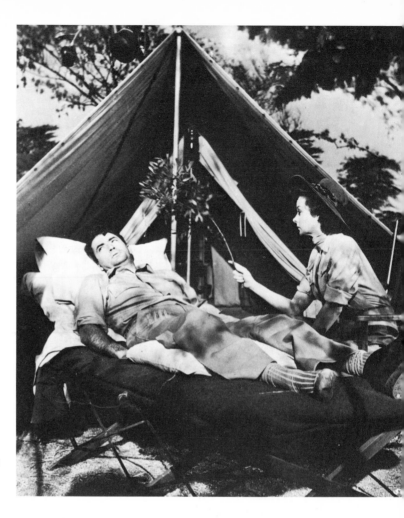

Coming to terms with death.
Gregory Peck and Susan Hayward in
Henry King's film version of 'The
Snows of Kilimanjaro', 1952.

mountain 'wide as all the world, great, high, and unbelievably white in the sun' – is softened to a rescue, a successful piece of surgery, Harry ready for the 'new start'. But the ending as written is immeasurably more powerful: though there is no hope of regeneration, Harry faces his failure to serve both art and life without self-pity, with understanding, submission to destiny, having at last 'burnt the fat off his soul'. Harry can be taken as a kind of Fitzgerald who has been endowed with the stoic insights of a Hemingway, but he can also be taken as a kind of Hemingway corrupted by the attractions of the role of man of action, neglecting his true vocation while the vultures and hyenas of devouring time close in.

The second African story is called 'The Short Happy Life of Francis Macomber' (filmed in 1947 with Zoltan Korda as director and Gregory Peck, Joan Bennett and Robert Preston in the leading roles), and it is simpler, less distinguished work of narrative art than the other, though unquestionably satisfying quintessential Hemingway. If 'Kilimanjaro' is about guilt, 'Macomber' is about fear, which may be termed a simpler and more universal emotion. Francis Macomber is a rich young American with a beautiful wife; both are on safari with a white hunter, very British, named Wilson. Their ways of designating each other are disarmingly straightforward: Macomber is a 'bloody coward', his wife a 'bitch', Wilson an 'insolent bastard'. Macomber runs away from a wounded lion, and the sense of the failure of his manhood is compounded by Wilson's cuckolding of him. But it is the insolent bastard who teaches the bloody coward the hunter's code of honour, whereby doubt and apprehension must be cut off by an act of will and physical action engaged in mindless physicality. Macomber overcomes his bloody cowardice but is shot by his bitch of a wife, who learns a kind of parody of the hunter's code (though she

Hemingway with admirers and a silver marlin in Havana Harbor, 1934.

Pauline on board the *Pilar*. The year
is 1934.

offends against it by firing from a car), but he dies purged of fear, his
new life indeed short but happy. The ancient Romans used to say
semper aliquid novi ex Africa: for Hemingway there was a new and
profound fictional theme – the value of insight learnt at the point of
death, a means of conquering death perhaps more satisfying than
coldly administering it. Fitzgerald was cracking up, but Papa the artist
– and, indeed, the proto-existentialist philosopher – was doing all
right.

He was also doing all right in material terms. He was able to put
down an advance of $3,300 for a $7,500 diesel-powered 38-foot cruiser
made by the Wheeler Shipyard in Brooklyn, NY, having heard of the
fisherman's paradise of Bimini – forty-five miles from Miami – and
needing a boat to get there. This boat was christened the *Pilar* – named
for the Spanish shrine but also for Pauline, who had used Pilar as a
secret code nickname when first courting Ernest. Great fisherman,
great writer, this same or different Ernest became one of the tourist
attractions of Key West, drinking in dungarees in Sloppy Joe's, a
man's man, an amiable bully, fit, brown, muscular, ready to fight
gloved or barefisted, hero of *Esquire* readers but held in some scorn by
the new and highly articulate forces of the American intellectual left.

He had, it was felt, let the progressives down. In the time of the
Great Depression he had hunted lions and marlin and gone to
bullfights, but he had written nothing in support of the chiliastic
doctrines of the revolutionaries. He had seen the left wing come to
power in Spain, but he had seen, so he said, no betterment in the lot of
the ordinary Spanish citizen. He did not feel any particular obligation
to democratic society, except to tell it the truth as he saw the truth. He
insisted that politics had nothing to do with art. The American left
wing was not too happy that Hemingway was popular in Russia – as
he still is. I was in Leningrad when the news of his death came
through, and the girls at the reception desk of the Astoria were crying
frankly. 'We were all the lovers of Yernyest Gyemingvay,' they said.
When Hemingway learned how much the Russians loved him, he
reiterated how little matters of ideology counted when it came to true
literary judgments. He was, one thinks, right.

He was, however, impelled to issue something that had the flavour
of a political statement at the time of the Great Hurricane in August
1935. This was a disaster that merely fingered Key West, leaving the
Pilar bucking but safe in churned waters; the real devastation was done
at Key Largo, Islamorada, Upper and Lower Matecumbe Keys.
Hemingway was anxious to get to the scenes of disaster and give what
help could be given, and in the boat of a sailor named Bra Saunders he
made Lower Matecumbe. What he found was horrifying. Following
President Roosevelt's 'pump-priming' policy, public works for war

veterans had been in progress on the Florida peninsula, and the workers lived in camps. The hurricane killed about a thousand of these workers, as well as a great number of fishermen and Floridians engaged in the tourist trades. The horror was summed up for Hemingway in one particular sight – two girls who had run a filling-station, now dead, 'naked, tossed up into trees by the water, swollen and stinking, their breasts as big as balloons, flies between their legs.' But the left-wing press saw in the sheer abstract number of dead workers, crammed together in a camp without adequate protection from the rage of the elements, a powerful argument against government callousness and inefficiency. The magazine *New Masses* wired Hemingway for an article about the disaster, and he responded with a bitter attack on the Washington bureaucrats.

This article – 'Who Murdered the Vets?' – seemed to many to be a sign of Hemingway's conversion to the revolutionary cause, but he was quick to say in private that his willingness to write for *New Masses* indicated no change of heart towards a pack of reds and pinks that had condemned his work consistently as 'socially unaware' but had been all too ready to run to him, who had had the guts to go and see the hurricane disaster for himself, when they wanted a dollop of palpitating truth. As for one of their editors, a certain Robert Forsythe who had treated his writings with exemplary scorn, he was very willing to smash the bastard's jaw the next time they met. On the other hand, a decent young left-winger sent Ernest an earnest letter begging him to write about justice and truth and give up his tough lonely stoics, and he got a gracious reply saying that the author would think about it.

He did, in fact, think about it. He went further: he actually produced a novel with a measure of 'social awareness' in it. This was *To Have and Have Not* (1937), his only novel with an American setting, whose very title proclaims its author's consciousness of injustice and inequality in the world. But no work was ever more unsuitable for adoption by the left wing as a piece of neat propaganda for collective reformist action. The hero is Harry Morgan, who had already been appearing in a new sequence of short stories as a hard-bitten loner and whose lineaments must, for filmgoers, be eternally those of Humphrey Bogart, as Mrs Morgan must forever be Lauren Bacall (or Mrs Bogart). Harry Morgan, despite his name, is no pirate, but he is presented as an unscrupulous decent man with a boat for hire, as ready to accommodate a fishing expedition as to murder a Chinese smuggler. He is a lone man and also a cheated man, and perhaps the one has something to do with the other. The big theme of early Hemingway was the possibility of a man's working out his salvation alone, concluding a 'separate peace', but the Hemingway of the late 'thirties

Hemingway, exposing government malpractice in a left-wing periodical, seemed to some to be at last abandoning political neutrality.

Humphrey Bogart and Lauren
Bacall in the film version of *To Have
and Have Not*.

seems now not to be too sure of this philosophy. Morgan says at one
point: 'I've got no boat, no cash, I got no education. . . . All I've got is
my *cojones* to peddle,' but his dying words, much-quoted, are: 'One
man alone ain't got no bloody f – ing chance.' This became a kind of
slogan to those members of the American left who, for prestige if for
nothing else, wanted Hemingway as one of themselves.

Unfortunately, Morgan is totally without 'social awareness' of the
orthodox kind. He can get along in the world only by using violence
(which the left innocently believed to be the monopoly of the right);
like any capitalist he does everything for profit. When the young
Cuban revolutionary Emilio rants about the tyranny of imperialistic
capitalism, he yells: 'The hell with their revolutions. All I got to do is
make a living for my family and I can't do that. Then he tells me about
his revolution. The hell with his revolution.' The people who prevent
his making a living are various and, in left-wing terms, ill-assorted –
the rich man who cheats him, the revolutionary who betrays him, the
US revenue officer who shoots him. If Morgan had money, he would
make his separate peace quickly enough. But presumably many left-
wing well-wishers had a cosy image of a Harry disgruntled and
thwarted enough to be willing to hear a Marxist homily or read a
pamphlet about the principles of dialectical materialism. And,
certainly, he is surrounded by enough of the wrecks of capitalist society

to justify the view that Hemingway was indulging in a snarl as political as that of 'Who Murdered the Vets?'.

On 18 July 1936 the Spanish Civil War erupted. Hemingway was at the time arranging a hunting trip in Wyoming, and he had plans for another fishing expedition to Bimini as well as another safari among the green hills. Still, he admitted that Spain was where he ought to be, and a good number of his fellow-Americans, who had no intention of going to Spain themselves, thought so too. Just after Thanksgiving, Walter Winchell the gossip columnist mentioned in his gossip column that gossip had it that old Papa was going out there to the war. The general manager of the North American Newspaper Alliance, NANA, read this piece of gossip, wrote to Hemingway that his organization was syndicated in sixty big newspapers, and invited him to cover the conflict. Hemingway said yes, but Pauline advised against it. Her intuition was telling her not that Ernest was going to get himself killed but that something nearly as apocalyptical was going to come out of that war – the death of their marriage.

For in this same month of December, Hemingway, dirty, in ragged shorts and torn T-shirt, was having a drink in Sloppy Joe's when two ladies came in, on vacation from St Louis. They were handsome and elegant, mother and daughter. The mother introduced herself as Edna Fischel Gellhorn, widow of an Austrian gynaecologist, and her daughter as Martha. Martha had been educated at Bryn Mawr and had published a novel and a book of short stories. She and Hemingway thus had literature in common, as well as a particular admiration for one of its more virile practitioners, and they could also talk animatedly about life in St Louis. Martha Gellhorn was sharp, intelligent, well-informed in world politics, and greatly concerned about the situation in Europe. She had been to Germany; she intended to go to Spain. She had a powerful desire to lash the smug democracies into an awareness of the dangers of militant fascism. She also had shining yellow hair that reached to her shoulders and the swaying grace of a movie star. Like most fiercely independent women who happen to be beautiful, she found her beauty something of a nuisance: it gave men the wrong idea. Whether Hemingway's ideas were wrong or right, he was certainly, as Pauline was grimly aware, attracted. When her mother went home Martha stayed on. Fortunately he was hard at work on *To Have and Have Not* and could not show her the fulltime attention that natural courtesy dictated. But when she left for Miami to catch the northbound train, Hemingway discovered that he had a pressing business engagement in New York which entailed his taking the same train. He and Martha dined in Miami and then, chugging north, continued their conversations about literature and St Louis. Pauline

Hemingway and Martha Gellhorn – the third Mrs Hemingway – loaded with hunter's loot in Sun Valley, late 1930s.

divined what was going to happen; it had happened in the same way ten years before.

In New York Hemingway signed his contract with NANA and helped to write the commentary for a documentary film, raw Loyalist propaganda, called *Spain in Flames*. But in his conversation and letters he emphasized that he was not taking political sides: he was concerned with humanity and the danger to humanity being signalled by the Spanish War. If he had known it at the time, he would doubtless have quoted that Meditation of the Dean of St Paul's, waiting in the *Oxford Book of English Prose* to be eventually rifled for a title, about no man being an island. And yet he stressed that he did not want to see the United States involved in a European war. Then he counted his traveller's cheques and set sail for Spain. Soon he was in Madrid.

Having dispatched his story about the Loyalist victory over the Italians at Guadalajara and Brihuega, having inspected the Madrid defences and found them adequate, having asserted that General Franco would never take the capital, Hemingway was ready to be hospitable to Martha Gellhorn, who arrived in Madrid ostensibly as war correspondent for *Collier's* but was, in fact, a very independent observer. Her independence recoiled at the patronage of Papa's greeting: 'I knew you'd get here, daughter, because I fixed it so you could,' a thumping lie. But Hemingway was always very possessive about Spain.

Despite his prophecy about the inviolability of Madrid, the city was soon under constant bombardment from Franco's artillery on Mount Garabitas. There was little sleep in the Hotel Florida, where the correspondents were billeted, and little to eat either. But Hemingway was always a welcome guest at the feasts of caviare and vodka that went on at Gaylord's Hotel, the Russian headquarters, and, while most were starved of transport or petrol as well as food, Hemingway never found any difficulty in getting about. He was, of course, having the time of his life. He was also working. Besides the dispatches he sent off to NANA, there was a film to be made with John Dos Passos – *The Spanish Earth*. This meant following the Loyalist tanks and infantry with the camera and running into genuine danger. But there was danger enough even in the Florida. A Rebel shell hit the hot-water tank there, and, as guests in night attire rushed from their bedrooms, a number of unsuspected liaisons were revealed. The most notable, though not unsuspected, was that between Hemingway and Martha.

We have to keep reminding ourselves that Hemingway had never shot, nor would ever shoot, another human being. Yet there was

The battle for Madrid, 1936. The aftermath of street fighting, one of the visual motifs of the next ten years in Europe.

Hemingway during the making of the Republican propaganda film *The Spanish Earth*. It was produced by a group called *Contemporary Historians*, amongst whom were John Dos Passos, Lillian Hellman, Archibald MacLeish and Hemingway himself.

something about his bearded bulky warrior's look that made the Eleventh and Twelfth International Brigades regard him as one of themselves. His trigger-finger itched, but only for innocent woodland creatures. One morning he shot a mallard, a partridge, four rabbits, and an owl. The owl was a mistake: he had thought it to be a woodcock. For the rest, he remained in increasingly dangerous Madrid as a convivial man of words, able to leave when he wished. He left when the footage of *The Spanish Earth* had been boxed and shipped, promising to be back, promising also to propagandize to the limit for the Loyalist cause.

His limit was extremely limited. Public speaking was the only activity of which he ever expressed terror. But he said a few words in Paris at Sylvia Beach's bookshop (Joyce was there, silent, apolitical, waging his own word-war within) and, in New York, addressed the Writers' Congress, asserting that fascism was intolerable to any man of letters who refused to lie. *The Spanish Earth* was finished and shown, with Hemingway's terse commentary, in influential places. It was even shown in the White House, which, in Hemingway's view, was presided over by a man without *cojones*. Hemingway, with a sufficiency of drink inside him, barked away for the Loyalists at Hollywood parties, and then took the hat round. Thousands of ciné-dollars poured into the ambulance fund, very helpful and discreetly non-belligerent. Then Hemingway went back to Spain.

Back in Madrid he was also back with Martha. There had as yet been no open break with Pauline, who wanted to save the marriage. Spain was two-thirds under the heel of Franco but the Loyalists were fighting hard and had taken Belchite; the arduous trip made by Ernest and Martha to the Belchite sector (they were the first American correspondents on the spot) was not conducive to dalliance. Martha proved a good pal and a brave woman. His admiration grew steadily. Madrid was quieter than on his previous visit, and he found time to memorialize the time, the place, and this tall blonde handsome girl in the play, his first and last, he called *The Fifth Column*. The woman correspondent in the play, Dorothy Bridges, is clearly Martha Gellhorn, though she sometimes talks like Lady Brett; Philip Rawlings – massive, brave, addicted to booze and raw onions, working as a spy while pretending to be a correspondent – is a typical piece of Hemingway self-projection. The author fixes the time and place of authorship in his introduction to the published text:

Each day we were shelled by the guns beyond Leganés and behind the folds of Garabitas hill, and while I was writing the play the Hotel Florida, where we lived and worked, was struck by more than thirty high explosive shells. So if it is not a good play perhaps that is what is the matter with it. If it is a good play, perhaps those thirty some shells helped to write it. . . . When you came back and found the room and the play intact you were always pleased. It was finished and copied and sent out of the country just before the taking of Teruel.

Hemingway followed the Loyalists into Teruel and was duly kissed and hugged and drenched with new wine like a genuine victor. He was not taken for an American writer with vague progressive leanings; he was taken for a Russian military officer and, naturally, tickled to death. He and Martha spent Christmas in Catalonia, while Pauline, trying still to save her marriage and growing her hair to shoulder length as an item in her armoury, was in Paris applying for a visa to Spain. But then Hemingway himself was in Paris, his liver plaguing him, the doctors warning him off the drink, and there were wretched marital quarrels with Pauline threatening to jump out of the hotel window. Hemingway was filled with proleptic remorse, knowing that his second marriage must go the way of his first, snarling about the way in which his NANA dispatches had been cut or even suppressed (Catholic enemies?), tortured by his liver, wanting to write in Key West, wanting to be back in Spain, wanting Martha. He sought consolation in what he called his faith, but the Church had sided with the God-damn fascists. He stayed briefly in Florida, then was back in Spain, to see bitterly the Loyalists retreating on all fronts, to brood on his messed-up life, to send off what the nameless bastards of NANA termed very inefficient dispatches.

Hemingway Reports Spain

Since March 18, Ernest Hemingway has been reporting the Madrid battlefront for the North American Newspaper Alliance. The article below consists of passages selected from five of his dispatches. They have already been printed in various newspapers affiliated with the Alliance, but such publication has often been incomplete because of lack of space in many papers.—THE EDITORS.

Valencia, Spain

AS OUR Air-France plane from Toulouse flew down over the business section of Barcelona, the streets were empty. It looked as quiet as downtown New York on a Sunday morning.

The plane hit smoothly on a concrete runway and roared around to a stop before a little building, where, chilled through by our trip over the edge of the snow-covered Pyrenees, we warmed our hands around bowls of coffee and milk while three pistol-armed, leather-jacketed guards joked outside. There we learned why Barcelona looked so momentarily quiet.

A trimotor bomber had just come over, with two pursuit planes as escort, and had dropped its load of bombs on the town, killing seven and wounding thirty-four. Only by a half-hour had we missed flying into the dog-fight in which the insurgent planes were driven off by government pursuit ships. Personally, I didn't mind. We were a trimotor job ourselves, and there might have been confusion.

Flying low down the coast toward Alicante, along white beaches, past gray-castled towns or with the sea curling against rocky headlands, there was no sign of war. Trains were moving, cattle were plowing the fields, fishing boats were setting out and factory chimneys were belching smoke.

Then, above Tarragona, all the passengers were crowded over on the land side of the ship, watching through the narrow windows the careened hulk of a freighter, visibly damaged by shellfire, which had driven ashore to beach her cargo. She lay aground, looking against the sand in that clear water like a whale with smokestacks that had come to the beach to die.

We passed the rich, flat, dark-green fields of Valencia spotted with white houses, the busy port and the great, yellow, sprawling town. We crossed rice marshes, and up over a wild mountain chain where we had an eagle's view of civilization, and

The fact is that Hemingway was never a very good war correspondent. His fiction-writer's talent impelled him to invent, organize reality into aesthetic patterns, cultivate the 'impressionism' which Ford Madox Ford encouraged writers to carry over from fiction to real life. Truth, according to Ford, was not facts but vision – a view which justified suppression and distortion of facts, what ordinary people call lying. Hemingway's temporary masters wanted to know the facts of the Spanish War, and Hemingway dished up a kind of subfiction in which he was the central character. His reportage of both the Spanish War and the one that followed immediately after is still very readable, but readable in the way that his self-confessed fiction is. For Hemingway in his years of maturity and fame – as opposed to those more conscientious days when he was earning his living as a journalist – war reportage was clearly a minor form of fiction-writing, untouched by the superior strokes which he carefully reserved for his major fiction. Organizations like NANA in effect subsidized his gathering of material for serious books. They had to make do with second-best Hemingway; sometimes they resented this.

Back in America, Hemingway began to organize his Spanish experiences into a novel. There were distractions, of course. *The Fifth Column* was badly adapted by a screen-writer, Benjamin F. Glaser, for production by the Theatre Guild (no writer in America can be trusted to find his own way through the mazes of dramaturgy; there has always to be a hack to show him what he really meant). His definitive volume of stories came out, with *The Fifth Column* (1938) as he wrote it at its head: the range of Hemingway's formal and narrative gifts is here remarkably displayed. The European war began, as he had said it would. His marriage to Pauline limped on, but it was clear that it could not be mended. After four years of what Martha termed enjoyable sin, she and Hemingway were to be married quietly by a justice of the peace in the town of Cheyenne. The divorce on the grounds of his eventual desertion of Pauline took a long time to come through, granting him leisure to wrestle with his conscience over this matter of a second marital defection. He, a nominal Catholic, made Pauline's real Catholicism into an acceptable excuse for the final break: she could not have more children without danger; sexual congress, so the Church said, was primarily for having children. Hemingway also convinced himself that he desperately needed a daughter and that Martha would give him one. She did not, and it may be said that he never gave her time to try. The Key West house was henceforth to belong to Pauline. Hemingway's residence from the beginning of the European war until almost the end of his life was to be Finca Vigía, San Francisco de Paula, Cuba. Martha, when not acting as foreign correspondent, was to be its first mistress, though not its last.

Opposite: The Spanish Civil War in word and picture. *Above, The New Republic,* 5 May 1937. *Below,* government forces parade in the captured town of Teruel, January 1938. Hemingway's play about the war, *The Fifth Column,* 'was finished and copied and sent out of the country just before the taking of Teruel'.

Martha and Hemingway at temporary peace in New York.

For Whom the Bell Tolls was published in late 1940 and was a huge commercial success – even in England, where a bigger war than the Spanish was occupying people's minds. In America it was a Book of the Month, which meant a club edition of 200,000 copies, matched by a regular trade edition of 160,000. Hollywood moved in early, and Hemingway was offered $136,000 for the film rights. Edmund Wilson, whose long essay 'Hemingway: Gauge of Morale' may still be read in the collection *The Wound and the Bow*, saw in the new novel 'a romanticizing of some of the material, an infusion of the operatic, that lends itself all too readily to the movies'. In other words, Hemingway seemed to be making concessions. It was true that the 'popular' novel of the American 'thirties had absorbed certain Hemingway elements: what had once been experimental was now part of every second-rate novelist's technical inventory. But Hemingway had not overtaken himself, nor his imitators: if the early novels could still strike the reader with a sense of freshness and wholly original power, *For Whom the Bell Tolls* had no stylistic shocks and merely the expected stylistic felicities. The subject was compelling and the story could be separated from the words in which it was told. Hemingway saw this with no misgivings. When he first met the film star Gary Cooper – in Sun Valley, where they were both shooting at animals – he saw in him the actor who could play the hero, Robert Jordan. So, a little later, he was much concerned with the shape of Ingrid Bergman's ears, since he wanted her for Maria, and Maria is shorn by the fascists. He found her ears as perfect as the rest of her. The fictional reality, in other words, could be found as much in a well-made film as in the original verbal artefact. Hemingway the literary man had been subtly corrupted – perhaps less by money than by devotion to the Loyalists.

And yet the verbal artefact has considerable power, while Sam Wood's film, made in 1943, is nearly as banal as nearly every other Hemingway movie. Certain scenes and symbols have a classic ring today, nearly forty years after the book's first appearance – Maria and Jordan's night of love, the 'alliance against death', when the whole earth seems to move beneath them; the 'solid flung metal grace' of the bridge, which is the one link between the opposed forces and also, in a wider view, the way by which the new age of mechanical regimentation will overtake the old pastoral world of simple needs and loyalties. Robert Jordan is not altogether plausible – an intellectual, an American professor of Spanish, fighting for the Loyalists but as ignorant as Harry Morgan of Communist ideology. A good deal of

Gary Cooper as Robert Jordan in Sam Wood's film version of *For Whom the Bell Tolls*, 1943. Cooper was Hemingway's own choice for the role. Henceforth they were to be friends.

He lay there on the brown ,pine -needled floor of the forest, and the

wind blew in the tops of the pine trees . The mountain side sloped gently where
he
we lay but below it was steep and we could see the dark winding of the oiled road

through the pass . There was a stream along the side of the road and far
he saw
down the pass I could see a mill beside the stream and the falling water of the
hot
dam white in the summer sunlight .

" Is that the mill ?" he asked .

"Yes ."

" I do not remember it ."

" It was built since you were here . The old mill is further down ; much

below the pass ."
He photostated military
I spread the map out on the forest floor and looked at it carefully .
He looked over my shoulder .

" Then you cannot see the bridge from here ."

" No," he said ." This is the easy country of the pass where
where the road turns out of sight in the trees,
the stream flows gently . Below it drops suddenly and there is a steep gorge ."

" I remember ."

" Across this gorge is the bridge ."

" And where are their posts ?"

" There is a post at the mill that you see there ."
I took my glasses out of my shirt pocket and screwed the
boards
eye pieces around until the of the mill showed suddenly
he saw
clearly and I could see the wooden bench beside the door ; the huge
shed
pile of sawdust that rose behind the open where the circular saw was and

a stretch of the flume that brought the logs down from the mountain side

on the other bank of the stream . The stream showed clear and smooth looking in the
below the curl of the falling water
glasses and the spray from the dam was blowing in the wind .

" There is no sentry ."

"There is smoke comeing from the mill house ," he said .

the background history of the Spanish War reads too much like a textbook and is not well integrated into the main story. But Maria and the formidable Pilar are the two best-realized of all Hemingway's women characters. He tried, though without success, to make Maria into a personage as compelling as Tolstoy's Natasha; indeed, he had a kind of Tolstoyan ambition in wishing to present a panorama of love and war that could at least be mentioned in the next breath to *War and Peace* – preposterous but not ignoble. The dignity of the aim – to speak the truth about love and pain and courage on the traditional high romantic scale – has to be applauded. Devoted to the Loyalist cause, Hemingway remains sufficiently the objective artist to delineate the human faults of what the left-wing propagandists wished to see presented as an incorrupt and shining chivalry. *For Whom the Bell Tolls* is not propaganda but art, and like all art it promotes a complex, even ambivalent, attachment to its subject. The book taught thousands to love or hate Spain, but it could not leave them indifferent to the land, its people, its history.

Hemingway was satisfied with the book, and with its reception, but he could not fail to see that it consolidated the wrong sort of reputation. He was no longer the promising young apostle of the avant-garde, nor was he the established great man of American letters. Dr Nicholas Murray Butler, president of Columbia University, vetoed the Pulitzer Prize Advisory Board's choice of the book, making it clear that he believed it to possess little literary merit. The general public's acclamation meant large income tax as well as large sales. Like every mature author, he looked back with profound nostalgia on the days when it was a thrill to get a few poems into private print. The generation of which he was a junior member was dying all around him – Ford Madox Ford in 1939 (and young Thomas Wolfe too), Scott Fitzgerald in 1940, Sherwood Anderson, Virginia Woolf and James Joyce in 1941. In many ways he was glad to throw himself into a world remote from the sophisticated guilts and cafards of America and Europe. He went, with Martha, to China.

She, a married woman with a well-heeled though atrociously taxed husband of great fame, clung to her independence and was very ready to earn money of her own on journalistic assignments. Hemingway had the sensation of being dragged with her to China – not much of a honeymoon, he said – but he generated his own idiosyncratic responses to the new scene. He drank snake wine – rice wine with small snakes coiled at the bottom of the bottle – and bird wine (dead cuckoos at the bottom). Talking of Hong Kong, he said that the stabilizing element in any British colony was the British women, who kept life on a formal basis. The women had been evacuated from Hong Kong, and the morale was in consequence low. He saw as much as he could of the

Opposite: First typed version of the opening of *For Whom the Bell Tolls*. 'Obviously' Hemingway was the only person to write a great book about the Spanish Civil War, Cyril Connolly had suggested in 1937.

Martha and Hemingway in China, 1941. Hemingway: 'A country both wonderful and complicated.' Martha: 'Papa, if you love me, get out of China.'

army of the Kuomintang. He observed the Japanese devastation of Kunming and evidence of that Chinese imperturbability which derived from awareness of an ancient civilization and a vast population. He met Chiang Kai-Shek and his wife in Chungking and was, since they both wished to charm him, charmed. But he did not feel inclined to celebrate this massive scene of struggle and change in a work of fiction. He was an exotic writer, but not all that exotic.

When the United States entered the war, Martha, a very warlike person, wanted Ernest to do his bit. He was always, as he thought, ready to do his bit, but it always had to be on his own terms. He had never had to take orders from anyone, except briefly on the Italian front all those years back, and he could never see himself as other than a natural guerrilla leader, a commander of irregulars, an unkempt private army man with eclectic artillery and a large cache of bottles. He could also, of course, be a private navy man, and he managed to have the *Pilar* officially accepted as a kind of Q-ship, searching for Nazi submarines off the Cuban coast, armed with grenades for throwing down sub conning towers, crewed by fine proven unshaven men who didn't give a damn ('We owe God a death') and were devoted to the man they called Papa. There was too much of this Papa obsequiousness, said Martha. Moreover, Papa got drunk too often and did not wash enough. As for the *Pilar* and its unwashed drunken patrols, it was all an excuse to obtain rationed petrol for fishing trips. There was, of course, a good deal in this: Martha was altogether too sharp and Papa never had an adequate reply ready. As though in response to Martha's scornful attacks, the 'Crook Factory', as Hemingway proudly called it, was disbanded by Washington, and Caribbean counter-espionage was put in the hands of the FBI, whose agents in Havana laughed at Papa's ineffectual amateurism. He responded by dubbing them 'Franco's Iron Cavalry' because some of them were Irish Catholics and, ergo, fascists.

With the private navy disbanded and Martha ready to go and cover the war in Europe, Hemingway knew he was going to be as lonely as hell. He decided he had better get into the war, God knew how. It was, as was to be expected, the efficient warlike Martha who found a way. Roald Dahl, now famous as a writer of short stories, was at that time Assistant Air Attaché to the British Embassy in Washington. He told Martha that the RAF would be proud to have its exploits written up in some American magazine by an author of the status of Ernest: if Ernest would be willing to take on such an assignment, he could be set up in Britain as a person engaged in 'priority war business' and be allocated official air transportation to London. *Collier's* – the magazine for which Martha was covering the European war – was

The *Pilar*, ostensible vessel of war against Nazis as well as fish.

Hemingway at the Dorchester, Park Lane, London, in 1944. The war correspondent meets the press over breakfast – ham and eggs and whisky.

only too willing to arrange a contract. Hemingway signed it and, in his own idiosyncratic way, joined the war. He was joining it late: it was almost D-Day.

Joining it meant, first, settling in at the Dorchester on Park Lane. It meant meeting old friends and making new friends and going to parties with both. Big-bearded and swaggering, Hemingway went down well enough in London, inviting everyone to a friendly barefist bout or to take a swipe at his iron-muscled stomach, laying down the law about bullfighting, boasting about his Q-ship adventures, playing the great American writer. But, in the ambience of modest courage, the tough-guy stance did not always appeal. Britain had fought hard and suffered much. Hemingway had sustained a leg wound thirty years before and then gained his manumission – not, in this heroic period, much of a veteran record. He had been, and was again, a highly paid war correspondent choosing when to court danger and when to desert it. Compare him with another writer – George Orwell. Orwell had been a real fighter in Spain, in danger as much from the political treacheries on his own side as from the enemy's bullets. He had been unglamorously wounded and he was not well. But he quietly worked away in London at his ill-paid brilliant journalism, preparing to create new and terrible myths out of his disillusionment, while Hemingway basked and boasted, was a boor and a bore.

His hubris was swiftly punished. Coming home in the blackout from a riotous party, he was involved in a car accident which inflicted a severe head wound and heavy concussion. Martha, who had travelled to England by ship, the one passenger in a cargo of high explosives, arrived in London to find him in the London Clinic, waiting for her affection and compassion. She merely laughed with her old scorn, belittling the great warrior and berating the foolish drunkard. His third marriage was already beginning to collapse, but his fourth and last was in preparation. He had met a most charming blonde from Minnesota at the White Tower restaurant in Soho, a journalist working for the *Daily Express* and married to Noel Monks of the *Daily Mail*. This was Mary Welsh, soon to be the ultimate Mrs Hemingway. After Martha had demonstrated her lack of love in the London Clinic, the bandaged but ambulant hero began to pay court. He did this mostly in verse, reserving prose for the war.

It is hard for any British soldier who served out the whole five and a half years to work up enthusiasm about the brief and glamorous Hemingway saga. The true irksomeness of the soldier's lot derives not from danger but from boredom and frustration. He hangs about waiting for orders, and, when the orders come, they seem brutally callous or unutterably foolish or both. He lacks freedom to act. He lacks good food, good pay, good tobacco, the present love of a good woman. He would be only too happy to be let loose to run his own private army, swinging two water bottles at his waist, one filled with gin and the other with cognac. He is bound to see the few months of Hemingway's cavorting over Europe somewhat sourly. Here is a rich and famous man doing what the hell he likes and being praised for it. He ate and drank well and suffered neither frustration nor boredom. He fulfilled the boy's-book dream of being a guerrilla leader. He had the best of all wars – a short and sharp one shorn of responsibility. There is, of course, a contrary way of looking at Hemingway's war: he elected to serve the allied cause rather than the editor of a magazine; he sought danger in full awareness; he brought the purple of a rich individuality to what Evelyn Waugh described as a sweaty tug-of-war between teams of faceless interchangeable louts.

On 6 June 1944 an invasion fleet of over 4,000 vessels sailed from British southern ports for the Normandy coast. Hemingway landed, but, as was to be expected, Martha landed first. Back in England, he flew with the RAF to see how they intercepted the V-1 bombs which, on 12 June, had begun to be launched. On 18 June the Cherbourg peninsula was cut by the Americans. The battle for Europe was on. On 18 July Hemingway attached himself to one of General Patton's armoured divisions but, not liking it much, soon went over to General Barton's 4th Infantry Division. It was not long before he was involving himself in the war more actively than was thought proper for a war correspondent. In Ville-dieu-les-Poêles he defied the Geneva Convention by tossing three grenades into a cellar where SS men were said to be in hiding. He sent off dispatches to *Collier's* which were wildly inaccurate but full of life. His real mission, so he said, was to get information on the disposition of enemy forces and pass this on to the true, official, fighters. He was a one-man self-elected unpaid intelligence unit.

Hemingway's role in the liberation of Paris has been loudly sung; it will always be difficult to separate the hard truth from the poetry, but there is no doubt that, on 2 August, five days before the city was freed, he was at Rambouillet, functioning as an unofficial liaison officer between the French partisan patrols and the 5th Infantry Division, stationed then at Chartres. He was installed comfortably in two rooms at the Hôtel du Grand Veneur, eating and drinking well, interrogating German prisoners, building up his own body of irregulars. On the morning of 23 August General Leclerc arrived in Rambouillet, and Hemingway was among those requested to deliver intelligence reports to Leclerc's G-2. The general was, apparently, rude and told the irregulars to withdraw from the coming liberation, which was his affair and his only. 'A rude general is a nervous general,' wrote Hemingway, who christened the brave soldier 'that jerk Leclerc'.

Mary Welsh, the fourth and last Mrs Hemingway.

"An old Frenchman in a black hat, a boiled shirt and a dusty black suit, with a bunch of flowers in his hand, saluted each tank formally"

There were weary tank men and German machine guns and a guy who once sang with a good band— and there was a man who knew that "there should never be tired generals"

BY CABLE FROM FRANCE

THE G.I. AND THE GENERAL
by Ernest Hemingway

THE wheat was ripe but there was no one there to cut it now, and tank tracks led through it to where the tanks lay pushed into the hedge that topped the ridge that looked across the wooded country to the hill we would have to take tomorrow. There was no one between us and the Germans in that wooded country and on the hill. We knew they had some infantry there and between fifteen and forty tanks. But the division had advanced so fast that the division on its left had not come up, and all this country that you looked across, seeing the friendly hills, the valleys, the farmhouses with their fields and orchards, and the gray-walled, slate-roofed buildings of the town with its sharp-pointing church tower, was all one open flank. All of it was deadly.

The division had not advanced beyond its objective. It had reached its objective, the high ground we were now on, exactly when it should have. It had been doing this for day after day after day after week after month now. No one remembered separate days any more, and history, being made each day, was never noticed but only merged into a great blur of tiredness and dust, of the smell of dead cattle, the smell of earth new-

broken by TNT, the grinding sound of tanks and bulldozers, the sound of automatic-rifle and machine-gun fire, the interceptive, dry tattle of German machine-pistol fire, dry as a rattler rattling; and the quick, spurting tap of the German light machine guns—and always waiting for others to come up.

It was merged in the memory of the fight up out of the deadly, low hedgerow country onto the heights and through the forest and on down into the plain, by and through the towns, some smashed, and some intact, and on up into the rolling farm and forest country where we were now.

History now was old K-ration boxes, empty foxholes, the drying leaves on the branches that were cut for camouflage. It was burned German vehicles, burned Sherman tanks, many burned German Panthers and some burned Tigers, German dead along the roads, in the hedges and in the orchards, German equipment scattered everywhere, German horses roaming the fields, and our own wounded and our dead passing back strapped two abreast on top of the evacuation jeeps. But mostly history was getting where we were to get on time and waiting there for others to come up.

Now on this clear summer afternoon we stood looking across the country where the division would fight tomorrow. It was one of the first days of the really good weather. The sky was high and blue, and ahead and to our left, our planes were working on the German tanks. Tiny and silver in the sun, the P-47s came in high in pairs of pairs and circled before peeling off to dive-bomb. As they went down, growing big-headed and husky-looking in the snarl of the dive you saw the flash and the smoke of the bombs and heard their heavy thud. Then the P-47s climbed and circled again to come down strafing, smoke streaming gray behind them as they dived ahead of the smoke their eight big .50s made as they hammered. There was a very bright flash in the trees of the wooded patch the planes were diving on, and then black smoke arose and the planes came down strafing again and again.

"They got a Jerry tank then," one of the tank men said. "That's one of the b——s less."

"Can you see him with your glasses?" another helmeted tank man asked me.

I said, "The trees hide him from this side."

"They would," the tank man said. "If we

(Continued on page 46)

ILLUSTRATED BY JOHN C. PELLEW

BATTLE for PARIS

BY ERNEST HEMINGWAY

CABLED FROM PARIS

Here is the first dispatch by Collier's correspondent, long a resident of the City of Light, on one phase of the swift drive into the French capital—and how impatient guerrillas joined in the fight for liberation

O N AUGUST 19th, accompanied by Private Archie Pelkey of Canton, in upstate New York, I stopped at the command post of the infantry regiment of the division in a wood just outside of Maintenon to ask for information on the front this regiment was holding. The G2 and G3 of this regiment showed me where their battalions were placed and informed me that their most advanced outpost was at a point a short distance beyond Epernon on the road to Rambouillet (23 miles southwest of Paris), where the summer residence and hunting lodge of the president of France is located. At the regimental command post I was informed there was heavy fighting outside of Rambouillet. I knew the country and the roads around Epernon, Rambouillet, Trappes and Versailles well, as I had bicycled,

walked and driven a car through this part of France for many years. It is by riding a bicycle that you learn the contours of a country best, since you have to sweat up the hills and can coast down them.

Thus you remember them as they actually are, while in a motorcar only a high hill impresses you, and you have no such accurate remembrance of country you have driven through as you gain by riding a bicycle. At the outpost of the regiment we found some Frenchmen who had just come in from Rambouillet by bicycle. I was the only person at the outpost who spoke French, and they informed me that the last Germans had left Rambouillet at three o'clock that morning but that the roads into the town were mined.

(Continued on page 83)

Opposite: Hemingway, unofficially fighting in a war, sometimes did the work he was paid for. *Left,* his eye-witness report of a great act of liberation (*below,* the Place de la Concorde, 1944). He personally 'liberated' the Traveller's Club and the Ritz.

Citizens and Allied war vehicles before the city hall (below) after liberation of Paris

PRESS ASSOCIATION, INC.

André Malraux, April 1945. Fellow-writers, fellow-liberators of Paris, he and Hemingway did not greatly care for each other.

Just after midday on 25 August, Hemingway was certainly in the Bois de Boulogne, in some danger from German machine-guns and shells, but equipped with a carbine and ready for two vinous 'liberations' – that of the Traveller's Club on the Champs Elysées and the Ritz in the Place Vendôme. He achieved both, took a room at the Ritz and, in a near-permanent haze of champagne and cognac, was ready to receive adoring visitors.

Mary Welsh was one of the first. That they loved each other was now common knowledge and one of the fruits of victory. André Malraux marched in, a full colonel in highly polished cavalry boots. Hemingway and he knew each other from the Spanish days, and Hemingway had never been able to forgive him for pulling out of the Civil War in 1937 – deserting the Loyalists to write huge 'masterpisses' like *L'Espoir*. Malraux now boasted of having commanded two thousand men while his friend Ernest had had a mere ragged handful. 'What a pity', Hemingway is supposed to have said, 'that we did not have the assistance of your force when we took this small town of Paris.' One of the partisans whispered to Hemingway: *Papa, on peut fusiller ce con?* The post-Hemingway generation of American writers was represented by Sergeant J. D. Salinger, whose work this great kind giant offered to look at. But, more than anything, Room 31 at the Ritz was consecrated to the joys of pre-marital love with Mary, brief but passionate, helped along by Lanson Brut.

Brief, because the war was not yet over for Hemingway. He attached himself to the 4th Division once more and drove with his old comrades into Belgium, observing and, in his own way, assisting in the hard battering of the Westwall. But then he was summoned to Supreme Headquarters, American Expeditionary Force, at Nancy. A certain Colonel Park informed him that grave accusations had been laid by his fellow-correspondents – to wit, that he had actively fought with the resistance, had run a headquarters complete with adjutant and map-room, had deliberately hidden his non-combatant insignia, had (and this was the bitterest and most malicious charge of all) impeded the orderly advance of the official forces by acting like one of the personages of his own fiction. He denied the charges, thus denying his own enterprise and near-heroism. His statement was made under oath, but he was prepared to go ahead with blatant perjury, though he was uneasy about this for many years to come. Had the charges against him been proved, the penalty would have been immediate repatriation and loss of accreditation as a war correspondent – no very severe punishment except for the loss of face involved and his exclusion from the final drive into Germany. He was acquitted and, somewhat shaken, retreated to the Ritz. Martha, typically, was now closer to the fighting than he was, her lovely hair gracing the forward division headquarters of the 82nd Airborne at Nijmegen. But Martha could go her own way now. Mary was with him in Paris, 'Papa's Pocket Rubens'. Marlene Dietrich was there too, some of the time, using the Ritz as a headquarters from which to conduct her famous husky singing forays into the front lines. And then Hemingway heard that the 4th Infantry Division was ready to launch a great offensive, and he wanted to be there.

He got to the Hürtengewald, a forest in the Rhineland where the Americans were preparing to clear out the firmly entrenched Germans and sweep a path clean for what, it was hoped, would be the final thrust of the war. By all accounts, Hemingway did well – brave, humorous, always in the thick of things, a father to the men, an elder brother to the officers. He endured three terrible weeks in which nearly three thousand casualties were reported in the regiment to which he was attached, but he saw the Germans beaten back. Tired and ill, he retreated once more to the Ritz, where he received Jean-Paul Sartre and Simone de Beauvoir, telling them with untypical generosity that William Faulkner was a far better writer than he. In bed, with a cold that would not leave him, periodically vomiting blood, he nevertheless perked up when he heard of the coming great offensive in the Ardennes – the Battle of the Bulge – which, he rightly divined, would be the final major battle of the West. He wanted to be with the 4th Division again, on the left flank of the American line, to see General von Rundstedt's armour make its last desperate thrust. He pulled strings, and was in Luxembourg in time for Christmas. A friendly colonel planned a little surprise for Hemingway: he invited Martha to spend the season of cautious rejoicing in the mess at Rodenbourg. The reunion was a disaster.

GIs meet their favourite author just before the Normandy landings.

Hemingway in Normandy, 1944 –
'brave Hemingstein', as he termed
himself.

Martha had already mentioned divorce in November. Now it was made publicly evident that the sooner the ill-matched couple parted the better. Martha scolded and taunted her husband; Hemingway treated her with the lordly condescension due from a real warrior to a mere camp-follower, though Martha had visited as many front lines as he. They saw a V-2 cutting through the air, and Martha, tough journalist as she was, noted time and place and said: 'Remember, Ernest, that V-2 is my story, not yours.' Ernest now began a period of savage vindictiveness and bad public behaviour, not only in Luxembourg but back at the Ritz in Paris. He transferred his enmity from Martha to Mary's husband, who apparently was putting obstacles in the way of her divorce, and he fired a machine pistol at his portrait – which Mary unfortunately had brought in her luggage – having first placed it on top of the toilet bowl. He howled with maniacal laughter and then delivered a long mad speech in excellent French to the management, standing on the bidet above the flooded bathroom. Mary now had a hint of what she was letting herself in for. Still, she was convinced she loved him. Hemingway had fired his last shot of the war (some have said his only one). The war was moving to its end and did not require his further assistance. It was time to go home.

Finca Vigía, or Lookout Farm, was an enclave of richness and order in an impoverished and decaying Cuban town. There were thirteen acres of flower and vegetable gardens, a cow pasture, an orchard, and a huge ceiba tree whose roots threatened to split the floor of the main house. There was a white frame guest house and a square tower intended as a working retreat, though it was primarily a home for the thirty cats of the establishment. There were three gardeners, a houseboy, a chauffeur, a Chinese cook, a carpenter, two maids, and a man who looked after the fighting cocks. There were dogs, including one called Black Dog that lay at the master's feet as he wrote. The next Cuban revolution was not yet, in the late 1940s, quite ready to foment. He was happy there, with 'Miss Mary', as he anomalously called her. He said:

Character like me, the whole world to choose from, they naturally want to know why here. Usually don't try to explain. Too complicated. The clear cool mornings when you can work good with just Black Dog awake and the fighting cocks sending out their first bulletins. Where else can you train cocks and fight them and bet those you believe in and be legal? Some people put the arm on fighting cocks as cruel. But what the hell else does a fighting cock like to do? . . . You want to go to town, you just slip on a pair of loafers; always a good town to get away from yourself; these Cuban girls, you look into their black eyes, they have hot sunlight in them. . . . A half hour away from the *finca* you've got your boat set up so you're in the dark-blue water of the Gulf Stream with four lines out fifteen minutes after you board her.

The beginning of the Peace: Finca Vigía, or Lookout Farm, near Havana. *Above:* With Christopher Columbus; the cats were so numerous that they had a house to themselves. *Below:* With Mary.

He was happy but, to his admirers, a spent literary force. He had produced nothing substantial since *For Whom the Bell Tolls*. He had written a great deal of a rather bad novel and then, suddenly aware of its badness, had abandoned it. He had not brought to any kind of imaginative order the mass of war experience he had accumulated in notes and memory. He was getting on for fifty but was not ready for silence. It was out of the need to stimulate his creative imagination into action that he left his acres of fighting cocks and daiquiris in the Floridita bar and returned to Europe, mother of all art. Venice became his new mistress, though he believed, having spilled his blood in Northern Italy so many years before, he had an ancient proprietary claim on her. He and Mary settled happily in the Venetian winter on the island of Torcello, later in Cortina. He shot duck and partridge, he tried to write. He needed, though he did not yet know it, the rejuvenating spark of a relationship with a surrogate daughter – autumnal, deciduous, minimally tinged with the erotic, painfully delicious. He found it with a nineteen-year-old girl called Adriana Ivancich, soft-voiced, devoutly Catholic, feminine with a femininity that was fast disappearing from America. His attitude to her seemed to him to be wholly paternal, but he made her the heroine of a novel in which the incestuously erotic unsuspected within him wantons in the wide bed of the imagination. The novel is *Across the River and Into the Trees*.

Hemingway, Mary and Rocky and Gary Cooper. A matter of some concern in Sun Valley, 1946.

General Stonewall Jackson, just before he died, spoke of crossing over the river and resting under the shade of trees. If we know the reference, we know what the novel is going to be about – an old soldier knowing that he is about to die. Hemingway's old soldier, Colonel Richard Cantwell, is not all that old – only his creator's age – and he dies of a heart attack, not in battle. He dies, moreover, in Venice, surrounded by images of life and evidence of the wonder of human imagination, loved also by a beautiful young contessa named Renata, one who is more than a girl, is indeed the tutelary goddess of the city itself. Hemingway is at his old game of planting death in the middle of life (death in the afternoon is enacted in the centre of the teeming vinous amorous city), reconciling himself to death by presenting it as part of life's cycle. He is also attempting to make art out of a theme which, badly handled, cannot but be sentimental, though well handled it can be Shakespearean, Sophoclean, Joycean – the weary father-lover and the radiant daughter-mistress. A book about an old woman loving a boy is either comic or disgusting; an old man loving a girl provokes wholesome lending-library tears or the crepuscular frissons proper to high romance, even tragedy. The *Times Literary Supplement* kindly discerned a Shakespearean quality in Hemingway's story, as did John O'Hara in the *New York Times*, but the majority of reviewers found mostly bad taste, stylistic ineptitude, and sentimentality.

There is, in fact, a failure of balance in the book. The images do not work. The body of the white wine the lovers drink is 'as full and lovely as that of Renata', which is silly. There is heavyhanded employment of military imagery in the erotic passages which, elegant in eighteenth-century pornography, is here very embarrassing ('Please attack gently and with the same attack as before'). The characters are not allowed merely to do the most elementary things, like closing a car door or reaching for the champagne or chewing a steak: they have to do them 'well' or 'accurately' or both. There are too many irrelevant snarls – at Sinclair Lewis, for instance, who meant Hemingway no harm and could not help his pockmarked face; at Martha Gellhorn (in thin disguise as Cantwell's third wife) – and these naturally hinder the reader's desperate attempt to find the Hemingway persona sympathetic.

On the other hand, I know of no modern novel – with the possible exceptions of Waugh's *Brideshead Revisited* and Aldington's *Seven Against Reeves* – that pays such eloquent homage to Venice. Hemingway rarely fails when he evokes the stone and waters, the views of Torcello and Murano from the lagoon, the cold mornings, the shops and the market, the esculence of the city. Leave Hemingway's senses alone, and they will function with fine animality, registering smell and

The Hemingways in Venice, 1949. Venice, said Hemingway, was absolutely God-damned wonderful. *Opposite:* In the Venetian Lagoon he prepares to kill something, probably duck. *Below left:* With Mary in Cortina d'Ampezzo. *Below right:* Adriana Ivancich, prototype of Renata in *Across the River and Into the Trees.*

sight and sound with a verbal accuracy that is a great wonder. Once let thought enter – which means trite philosophizing and, worse than anything, Hemingway's notion of himself as stricken hero – and the prose falters, the images collapse, the reader reddens with embarrassment or the effort to contain his derision.

Handling the first edition of the novel now, one is moved, against one's will, by the dust-cover design, which was done by Renata's original, Adriana Ivancich. There is a real-life situation memorialized there far more affecting than Hemingway's attempt to turn it into art. Mary, the good wise wife, saw what was happening to Ernest and was sympathetic. It was the last twitch of unrealizable desire for youth. The middle-aged man aches to be reborn (*renatus* in Latin, feminine *renata*) but knows it is too late. What gives Joyce's *Finnegans Wake* its wholly human appeal – missed all too often by readers who regard it as a mere verbal fantasia – is the hopeless desire of its hero Earwicker, another man of fifty, for a daughter who can never be a mistress. *Incest* becomes *insect* in his dream, tragic Earwicker a comic earwig; a comic history of the world, a chronicle of great men falling into forbidden love, enfolds the sin that Earwicker dare not commit. Hemingway was not as big as Joyce: he could not flash humour on to his predicament. He began to grow old with an ill grace.

Late 1950 was a bad time. The critics shook their head at *Across the River and Into the Trees* and said Hemingway was done. But his response, apart from the usual outraged snarls and offers to crack heads, was to work hard in an effort to show that he was far from done. He was writing a long 'sea novel' (to be published, as we know, posthumously and to general critical glumness as *Islands in the Stream*) and exulting in an ability to pour out words which, so he told Adriana, owed everything to her. This was back at the Finca, where Adriana and her mother were visiting. He had converted the daughter and dream-mistress into a muse, a classical and healthy process. The sea novel was to have four long sections, three of which already had provisional titles: *The Sea when Young, The Sea when Absent, The Sea in Being*. By the autumn of 1951 he had got the vast mass of words pared down to what was still a very sizable novel.

And yet he decided against publishing it. He gave too many reasons – tax would eat up his profits, some of the book was highly personal, he wished to revise but not yet. Perhaps his real reason was awareness of the book's comparative dullness and stylistic mediocrity. But there was one section of it that he was prepared to peel off and publish as a brief self-contained entity. This was the novella to be called *The Old Man and the Sea* – a book that gained him the Pulitzer Prize and restored his international reputation to the extent of his being considered worthy for the biggest prize of all, that sold immensely, that moved ordinary

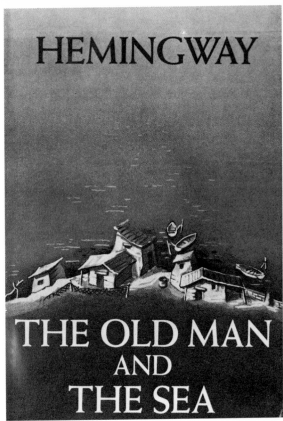

people to tears, that is unquestionably a small masterpiece. One of the mysteries of the creative process is exhibited in the circumstance that Hemingway could write so superbly at a time when he was writing so indifferently. The little book appeared in 1952 (again with a cover designed by Adriana), having first been published in a single issue of *Life* that sold over five million copies in forty-eight hours. Its impact was incredible. Sermons were preached on it, the author received a hundred laudatory letters every day, people kissed him, weeping, in the streets. His Italian translator could hardly translate for tears. As the hero was a poor Cuban fisherman, the Batista government (which Hemingway privately detested) awarded him a medal of honour 'in the name of the professional marlin fishermen from Puerto Escondido to Bahía Honda'. Film proposals were quickly under way. Hemingway was sardonic as ever about the inevitable cinematic butchering, though he greatly took to Spencer Tracy (the proposed star) as a human being. He was later to say that Tracy in the film looked like a fat Hollywood actor pretending to be a poor Cuban fisherman.

Into the last ten years: dust jackets of the first American editions of *Across the River and Into the Trees* (1950) and *The Old Man and the Sea* (1952).

Hemingway and Mary suitably posed against a background of Kilimanjaro – the mountain whose western summit, Hemingway wrote in 'The Snows of Kilimanjaro', is called by the Masai *Ngajè Ngajè*, the House of God.

It is easy to understand why the novella was, and continues to be, so universally popular. It is about courage maintained in the face of failure. An old man goes out in his boat and sights a great marlin. Like the matador with the bull, he feels drawn to the magnificent creature, so that, though one has to kill the other, he does not mind who kills whom. In an almost religious humility, old Santiago says: 'Never have I seen a greater, or more beautiful, or a calmer or more noble thing than you, brother. Come on and kill me.' His willingness to die in an act of worship gains him a reward: he kills the fish, though at once he is tortured by remorse: 'You killed him for pride and because you are a fisherman.' As he hauls the great fish home the sharks attack it: he is being punished for his hubris. He reaches land trailing a huge mutilated corpse. But Santiago has not, in his failure, really failed. He has shown a right pride and a right humility; he has dared and touched grandeur. 'Man is not made for defeat. A man can be destroyed but not defeated.' This simple tale is loaded, though not ostentatiously, with allegorical meanings which delighted the Sunday preachers. As an exercise in simple 'declarative' prose it is unsurpassed in Hemingway's œuvre. Every word tells and there is not a word too many; the long hours of learning the marlin-fisher's craft – wasted, escapist, reactionary

hours in the view of those left-wing voices now long silenced – had paid off. Writers must know about things as well as words.

It was a satisfied and fulfilled Hemingway who set off for Africa again, first calling at Pamplona. He had done no boasting, but life began to behave as though he had. He shot well, as did Mary. He was made, to his pleasure, an Honorary Game Warden in the Kimana Swamp territory of Kenya. On 21 January 1954 they took off from West Nairobi airport in a small plane piloted by a young man called Roy Marsh, their aim being to take a trip to the Belgian Congo. Over Murchison Falls on the Victoria Nile a flight of ibis crossed the path of the aircraft. Marsh dove to avoid them and struck an abandoned telegraph wire that stretched over the gorge. The propeller was hit. He lost height steadily and crashed in a thorn thicket three miles south-west of the Falls. Ernest sprained his right shoulder and Mary was in profound shock. Otherwise nobody was hurt. The wireless did not function, there seemed no hope of overland rescue. After a night on a hill, dozing by a fire, they saw a white boat named the *Murchison* tying up at a landing-stage on the great river. They signalled, shouted, descended. A canny Indian was in charge of the vessel, one well used to rich Americans. He had rented his boat to John Huston during the

Hemingway in camp with Philip Percival, whose courage he had acknowledged in *Green Hills of Africa*, and a friend unidentified. *Below:* the aircraft in which he crashed.

Ava Gardner, star of *The Killers* and
'The Snows of Kilimanjaro', one of
the large tribe of Hemingway
'daughters'.

filming of *The African Queen*. He demanded fares of one hundred shillings per passenger. As a Len Deighton character says, there's no business *but* show business. The three were taken to Butiaba on the eastern shore of Lake Albert, there to learn that the news was already buzzing of the death of Ernest Hemingway (and, incidentally of course, his wife and pilot). A BOAC Argonaut had spotted the wreckage but no sign of survivors.

And now the incredible happened, proving that lightning always strikes the same tree twice. They arranged to be transported in a twelve-seater De Havilland Rapide from Butiaba to Entebbe and did not even achieve take-off. The plane, which seemed moderately airworthy, bumped over an airstrip full of stones and furrows, lifted, dropped, lurched, fell, burst into flames. Hemingway butted a jammed door open with his head and damaged shoulder. Roy Marsh kicked out a window and got himself and Mary through. Hemingway wrote:

There were four small pops representing the explosion of the bottles of Carlsberg beer which had constituted our reserve. This was followed by a slightly louder pop which represented the bottle of the Grand MacNish. After this, I clearly heard a louder but still not intense explosion which I knew signified the unopened bottle of Gordon's gin. This is sealed by a metal cap and therefore gives an explosion of greater power than that of the Grand MacNish which is only sealed by a cork and, in any event, had been half consumed. I listened for further explosions but there were none.

Tradition has it that Hemingway emerged from the accident waving a bunch of bananas and a bottle of gin and shouting: 'My luck she is running very good.' A popular song with this refrain was recorded by Rosemary Clooney and her husband José Ferrer shortly afterwards. It begins with the sound of a plane crashing and goes on to treat the African adventure in conventional comic terms. Actually, despite Hemingway's attempt to make light of it, he, if not Mary, was very badly injured. He was even, despite the congratulatory cables and premature obituaries (which are supposed to give their subject a new lease), in danger of death. The catalogue drawn up in Nairobi specified grave overall concussion, temporary loss of vision in the left eye, loss of hearing in the left ear, paralysis of the sphincter, first degree burns on face, arms and head, a sprained right arm and shoulder and left leg, a crushed vertebra, and a ruptured liver, spleen and kidney. As if all this were not enough, he helped, a month later, to put out a bush fire and fell into it, emerging with second degree burns on his legs, belly, chest, lips, left hand and right forearm. Thereafter he waited quietly in Mombasa until it was time to board the ship to Venice. Venice, he felt, would put him right.

A. E. Hotchner, one of his new friends and eventual biographers, was appalled by the change in him:

When I came into his room he was sitting in a chair by the windows, reading, the inevitable white tennis visor (ordered by the dozen from Abercombie & Fitch) shading his eyes. He wore his crumpled wool bathrobe and the GOTT MIT UNS leather belt. . . . I stood for a moment in the open doorway, shocked at his appearance. . . . What was shocking to me now was how he had aged in the intervening five months. What there was of his hair (most of it had been burned off) had turned from brindle to white, as had his beard; and he appeared to have diminished somewhat – I don't mean physically diminished, but some of the aura of massiveness seemed to have gone out of him.

He had contrived his own therapy – chilled champagne and a couple of slices of obituary every morning, bed in the afternoon and pills by the handful, plans for going to Spain by car. He was in great pain but determined to go on drinking life to the limit, with *drinking* the just word. But the glamour of his past life kept supervening on the pedestrian present, which could only be moulded to the glamorous when it became the past. He was full of tales of his past, and not all of them could be believed. In 1965, for instance, Caedmon Records of New York put out a long-playing disc called *Ernest Hemingway Reading*, on which one of his lying stories is committed to posterity, the notorious one that Hotchner and others heard live. It concerns Mata Hari.

Ingrid Bergman, Maria in the film version of *For Whom the Bell Tolls* and also one of Hemingway's adopted 'daughters'.

He told a well-wined group of us that he did not know her very well, since he was a simple sublieutenant and she was consorting with general officers and Cabinet ministers, 'but one night I fucked her very well, although I found her to be very heavy throughout the hips and to have more desire for what was done for her than what she was giving to the man.'

Hemingway, as we know, first went to Europe in 1918. Mata Hari had already been shot for espionage the year before.

He did not have to lie about his present fame. Driving through Piedmont on the second lap of the journey to Madrid (the first lap had taken him to Milan, where he revisited Ingrid Bergman and expressed scorn for her common-law husband, the great film director Roberto Rossellini), he was mobbed by his admirers in the town of Cuneo. Nearly crushed by their enthusiasm, shaken and sick, he had his beard shaven off in Nice. Then on to Madrid and the bullfights and an affectionate reunion with Ava Gardner, who was in love with the torero Luis Miguel Dominguín. But he was tired and ill and had to go back home to Cuba.

In 1954 Hemingway received the Nobel Prize for Literature. It was an award he both wanted and did not want. After all, Sinclair Lewis, whose books, character, and appearance Hemingway alike execrated, and William Faulkner, whom he now seemed to regard as a bourbon-soaked verbalizer, had both been Prizemen. Moreover, 'no son of a bitch that ever won the Nobel Prize ever wrote anything worth reading afterwards,' he said before he got it. When he got it he found fault with the Nobel Committee's official citation, which saw him as a writer who had heroically come out of an early 'brutal, cynical and callous' phase to emerge as a kind of Marryat full of 'manly love of danger and adventure', with a 'powerful, style-making mastery of the art of modern narration'. The whole summation of his literary career seems inept, and the term 'style-making' sounds like a cybernetic rendering of a Swedish word that means something different (or at least means something: 'style-making' means nothing). Hemingway was glad of the cheque for $35,000: now wealthy, he had begun to play the part of a man in grave financial need. The gold medal he considered giving to Ezra Pound, who deserved all the literary medals that had ever been struck, but finally presented to the shrine of the Virgen de Cobre, Cuba's matron saint.

He was not well enough to go to Stockholm, but he said he would not have gone if fit, since he, who had never owned even a set of underwear, was not now going to invest in a dress suit. But the speech he wrote for delivery by the American Ambassador was well thought out and toughly gracious:

Writing, at its best, is a lonely life. Organizations for writers palliate the writer's loneliness but I doubt if they improve his writing. He grows in public stature as he sheds his loneliness and often his work deteriorates. For he does his work alone and if he is a good enough writer he must face eternity, or the lack of it, each day. For a true writer each book should be a new beginning where he tries again for something that is beyond attainment. He should always try for something that has never been done or that others have tried and failed. Then sometimes, with great luck, he will succeed. How simple the writing of literature would be if it were only necessary to write in another way what has been well written. It is because we have had such great writers in the past that a writer is driven far out past where he can go, out to where no one can help him. I have spoken too long for a writer. A writer should write what he has to say and not speak it. Again I thank you.

What gave him more pleasure than the Nobel Prize – whose aftermath was countless interviews and uninvited visitors – was the spontaneous tribute of affection and admiration accorded him by the crowd at a *corrida* in Zaragoza. Two bulls were dedicated to him; hundreds brought bullfight tickets to be autographed. His *Death in the Afternoon* was known to Spanish aficionados and taken as a lover's testament, a homage to the Spanish people as well as to their major secular ritual; his *For Whom the Bell Tolls* was banned by the Falangist régime, but the Spaniards knew about it and knew where Hemingway's heart lay. They saw him as an enemy of Franco too

Hemingway, posing for a portrait, proves that the hair on his chest is real.

powerful to be kept out of the land he loved. He looked powerful; in truth he was very ill.

His blood pressure and cholesterol count were perilously high, his liver was functioning atrociously (he did not help it by drinking as much as he did), his aorta was inflamed. He was warned off fat, alcohol, and love-making. Morose, he went to winter at the Ritz in Paris, where he made an astonishing and life-restoring find. There were two small trunks with his name on them which had been languishing in the Ritz cellars since 1928. In them were old longhand notes, abortive attempts at fiction and reportage dating from the good days. A fine book was to come out of the years of the Prizeman, despite his cynical snarl, but it was a book whose foundations had been laid, and stylistic felicities achieved, in the old days of struggle. It was to be published posthumously under the title of *A Moveable Feast*.

Back in Cuba the political situation was growing tense – too tense for an American expatriate writer whose guest status forbade his speaking out. A government patrol came prowling in the grounds of the Finca, searching for a rebel fugitive. They killed one of Hemingway's dogs, and the outraged master did not dare speak a

Hemingway and Castro, 1960: after twenty years in the country, the writer had told reporters the year before, he felt himself a true Cuban.

word. He exiled, or repatriated, himself to Ketchum, Idaho, and followed anxiously the news from Havana. He heard on 1 January 1959 that Fidel Castro had taken the capital and that Batista had run away to Ciudad Trujillo. He was glad: 'the Cuban people now have a decent chance for the first time ever.' He knew nothing of Castro but asserted that nobody could be worse than Batista. He saw clearly that American financial interests would oppose the new régime, that, as an American, he would henceforth be *persona non grata* in his adopted country. He worried about the Finca but was telephoned by an official of the new government, Jaime Bofils, that he was making the protection of the estate his personal responsibility. The Batista sergeant who had shot Hemingway's dog had been hanged and his corpse mutilated, though not for that particular crime. Still, things at the Finca could never be as they had been. Before going off to spend the summer in Spain, Hemingway bought a house in Ketchum. He could also have Key West again if he wished. Pauline was now dead. 'She died like everybody else,' said Hemingway, in response to Tennessee Williams's inquiry as to how she died. 'And after that she was dead.'

He spent his sixtieth birthday at La Consula, near Málaga, the estate of a wealthy American acquaintance. Mary arranged a magnificent party, with flamenco and fireworks and a great cake. The birthday king, whose kidneys were bad, was disclosing signs of more than physiological disorder. He snarled and sneered at his living wife as he had at his dead one. When a friend patted him affectionately on the shoulder and accidentally touched the back of his head, he yelled that that was one spot where nobody was allowed to touch him. He spoke of nothing but his romantic past and was gratuitously foul in his language. Mary, patient as a saint, had no good memories of this Spanish summer and was anxious to get back to Cuba or Idaho. But Hemingway had contracted to write a long article about bullfighting for *Life*, and Spain, he said, was the only place to write it. This article was to be aptly titled – *The Dangerous Summer*.

The article began to swell into a small book. He had to take it back to the Finca to finish it. All his fears of being booed out of Cuba as an unwanted alien were dispelled at Havana airport, where the entire population of San Francisco de Paula had turned out with banners to greet him. But he worried. 'I just hope to Christ the United States doesn't cut the sugar quota. That would really tear it. It will make Cuba a gift to the Russians. . . . The anti-United States is building. All around. Spooks you. If they really turn it on, I'm sure they will put me out of business.' The amount of work facing him – including the answering of ninety-two letters – made him, for the first time in his career, feel that he needed a secretary. He had met a Glasgow girl in Spain who might do. Should he import her? The *Life* article now stood at 63,562 words and had missed its deadline. His eyes were bad – 'Cornea is drying up. Tear ducts dried up already' – and the only book he could read was a large-type edition of *Tom Sawyer*. *The Dangerous Summer* reached 92,453 words.

The Dangerous Summer reached 108,746 words. Hemingway did not know how to cut it. Moreover, he felt he had to go back to Spain to check on certain things, such as the practice of shaving the bull's horns. He also needed certain photographs. He recognized that this was indeed a book. How much money could he make on such a book? He was worrying about money, though his royalty income was around $100,000 a year, his tax account was overstocked, his stocks and shares were ample and healthy. Twentieth Century-Fox wanted to buy ten Nick Adams stories and offered $100,000. 'Christ, that's what they paid for *one* story,' Hemingway screamed. '"Snows of Kilimanjaro", they paid that. . . . Once you set a price in Hollywood, you can't back down. They can have the ten stories for nine hundred thousand.' These, and similar, words were not spoken by a tough muscled fighter of a man but by a querulous whitebeard. Hotchner writes: 'His chest and shoulders had lost their thrust and his upper arms were macilent and formless, as if his huge biceps had been pared down by an unskilled whittler.'

At Yesa Dam, near Pamplona, July 1959.

Part of *The Dangerous Summer* appeared in *Life* – disappointingly repetitive and colourless writing, with a page of photographs that, in Madrid, drove Hemingway to an anger that his friends could not understand: 'The one labelled *pase ayudado* – hell, that's the kind of picture photographers use to blackmail bullfighters. . . . I'm the laughingstock of anyone who knows anything about bullfighting and has seen the piece. I'm regarded as the crook and double-crosser of all time. . . . Would rather be smashed up like in Africa any number of times than have the feeling that page of pictures gave me.' And so on, for hours. But nobody else could see anything wrong with the pictures. As for the new pictures Hemingway had obtained in Spain and was ready to take back to New York, he worried about the possibility of *Iberia* airline's having a rule against excess baggage and refusing to allow him to take them. He was reassured by Hotchner and others. 'Yes, but this midnight plane isn't a jet,' said Hemingway, 'and maybe they don't allow excess baggage on prop planes. If the photos don't go on, neither do I.' Hotchner finally had to obtain a written assurance from the *Iberia* manager that it was in order for a passenger to board with excess baggage. Hemingway folded this note and stowed it with care inside his passport.

Why was he taking a nonjet flight anyway – fourteen hours to the jet's seven? Because there was less chance of enemies looking for him on a nonjet. Because he preferred a fairly slow descent into the all-consuming drink, meet death at leisure. It seemed to his friends that Hemingway was moving towards dementia, and not at leisure either. Back in Ketchum he worried because his car lightly grazed another car: the sheriff would stick him in jail; the owners of that car did not really mean it when they said the damage was not worth arguing about. He said, in spite of the reassuring evidence of his bank statement, that he and Mary could not afford to keep on the Ketchum house. The 'Feds' were after him, he said. He had imported that Glasgow girl met in Spain into the United States and was paying for her course in dramatic training: the FBI would interpret that as a cover for gross immorality. Those two men working late at the bank were 'Feds', checking his bank account for irregularities. Those in the bar, over there, that looked like travelling salesmen, they were 'Feds' too: let's get out of here.

To persuade Hemingway to visit a psychiatrist was out of the question. But there were physiological disorders enough to convince him of the reasonableness of an examination by Dr Hugh Butt, a hepatic specialist, at St Mary's Hospital in Rochester, Minnesota. Butt found mild diabetes and hypertrophy of the liver – the penalty of a lifetime's hard drinking. He might conceivably have the rare disease called haemachromatosis, but a definitive diagnosis would require a

biopsy, which Dr Butt was not at present prepared to conduct. There
was hypertension, of course, and perhaps the drugs Hemingway had
been taking to control it were partially responsible for the depression
symptoms. Dr Howard P. Rome, who was a psychiatrist but did not
present himself as one to the patient, recommended and administered
a course of electric shock treatments.

In the New Year of 1961, Hemingway, a frail old man,
whitehaired, pale, meagre-limbed but apparently very much better,
was permitted to go home to Ketchum. He was asked to contribute a
sentence to a presentation volume for newly inaugurated President
John F. Kennedy, but a whole day's work produced nothing. 'It just
won't come any more.' He wept. Spring came, and Hemingway
seemed, preoccupied with some inner vision or with the coming
revelation of *nada*, to see nothing of it. He took a shotgun and two
shells. Mary, who suffered much and showed rare courage, talked to
him until his local doctor arrived to take his daily blood pressure. The
doctor persuaded Hemingway to hand over the gun.

The house at Ketchum, Idaho –
Hemingway's last home.

He had to be readmitted to hospital. Before getting into the car that was taking him to the airport he made a dash to the gunrack and put a loaded gun to his throat. Thwarted, he muttered all the time in the aircraft the word 'Shanghaied'. The aircraft landed, halfway to Rochester, for refuelling, and Hemingway, apparently sane enough, got out to stretch his legs. He searched frantically everywhere for a gun, even in the glove compartments of parked cars. He tried to walk straight into the path of another plane that was taxiing down the airstrip. Back with Dr Rome, he was put on his honour not to make another suicide attempt. His dementia took a very cunning form, wherein he presented the face of insanity to his wife and, to his doctors, the lineaments of sweet reason. Dr Rome, to Mary's horror, thought he could safely be discharged. Driving home to Ketchum, she found him starting his irrational fears again. They had a picnic lunch and drank wine: the state troopers, he was convinced, would arrest them for carrying alcohol. He worried about where they could spend the night: Mary must telephone to make reservations in motels that, she knew, would be totally empty. Back in Ketchum he was morose but seemed resigned to living.

On the morning of Sunday, 2 July 1961, he got up very early while Mary was still asleep, found the key to the storage room where the guns were, loaded a double-barrelled shotgun that he had used for shooting pigeons, and took it out to the front foyer of the house. When first speaking to Hotchner on the telephone he had introduced himself as 'Doctor Hemingway'. He that dies this year is quit for next. We owe God a death. In the story 'A Clean, Well-Lighted Place' there is the prayer: 'Our nada who art in nada, nada be thy name thy kingdom nada thy will be nada in nada as it is in nada.' He put the twin barrels to his forehead and fired. It woke the whole house up.

The most sizable of the books of Hemingway that were published posthumously is *Islands in the Stream**, which his widow and publisher decided to issue in 1970. They recognized that it badly needed revision but considered that the work had enough intrinsic merit to stand in the Hemingway œuvre. For students of Hemingway's tormented psyche it has its own interest. Professor Waldhorn says: 'As a formal work of art the novel cannot survive close analysis. But there is present in the work another kind of pain too, the torment of the author, whose personal experience is almost frighteningly transparent beneath his fictional distortions. What force *Islands in the Stream* has – and it is potent – lies just beyond the boundaries of the art of fiction.'

* Filmed in 1977, with George C. Scott as Thomas Hudson, directed by Franklin J. Schaffner.

The first, longest, and best section of the novel deals with the summer vacation of Thomas Hudson, a famous American painter, whose three sons are with him on the island of Bimini. Hudson is, apparently, much loved and respected by everyone, without having to exhibit any qualities of lovableness, though his respectability is never in doubt. He has done well in his art, though not in his two marriages. He supervises the ritual of his youngest sons' initiation into manhood, which takes the form of battling with big fish, a good father but somewhat remote, priestlike, no pal. The two sons go off after their holiday. After a few days Hudson receives a telegram telling him that they, with their mother, the second wife, have been killed in a car accident.

In the second part of the novel Hudson learns that his eldest son, a fighter pilot in the Second World War, has been killed in combat. The first wife, the mother, unexpectedly arrives. She is an actress cheering up the front-line troops, and she has a powerful resemblance to Hemingway's 'Kraut', Marlene Dietrich. She knows nothing of the death of her son. She and Hudson make love, and the bad news is casually imparted and as casually received. 'Tell me. Is he dead?' – 'Sure.' Then, in the third part, Hudson goes off to look for the survivors of a Nazi submarine sunk off the Cuban coast, leading a crew of six in his camouflaged yacht, obviously the *Pilar*. He succeeds, or tells himself he succeeds, in not thinking about his dead sons. Then he is wounded seriously – perhaps mortally: we are not permitted to be sure. Probably Hemingway was desperately superstitious about depicting what would in effect be his own death.

And yet Hudson, the successful, the loved and respected, thinks of little but death throughout the book. Hemingway has to justify this obsession through a variety of unconvincing devices – memories of a younger brother drowned, the coldly reported deaths of the sons, a war in which people expect to die. He even inserts dreams and nightmares which shunt Hudson's obsession to the level of the irrational. One dream presents Hudson apparently using a pistol as a penis and then wearily accepting the woman's role in the act of love. The tiredness, the death urge are Hemingway's own. We have a classic example of a work of fiction which, not wholly successful as art, does not sufficiently illuminate, either, the spiritual predicament of the creator, whose psychic torment has presumably led him to the attempted catharsis of a book.

What was wrong with Hemingway? Possibly growing gloom at his failure to be his own myth; more possibly a sexual incapacity which, considering his prowess in other fields of virile action, deeply baffled him. He always boasted of having *cojones*: but *cojones* have properly nothing to do with the ability to fire guns. There may have been a self-disgust at his inability to live up to his youthful, Joycean, ideal of total artistic dedication: he had become a mass of public muscle and, corrupted by the wrong kind of fame, found it too late to retreat. With fame, anyway, any kind of sense of recognized achievement, the incursion of a chronic melancholy may be expected, expressible as a death urge. Or, simpler, Hemingway saw himself as an exception to the Thoreauvian rule of, like all men, having to live a life of quiet desperation: he could not cope with the stress that most men endure gracefully; he was too godlike to be expected to have to cope.

A Moveable Feast, the reworked Paris notebooks that, after much patient hammering and filing, emerged as a kind of autobiography of the years of literary apprenticeship, appeared in 1964. The religious connotation of the title is as apt as that of *The Sun Also Rises*. The young Hemingway and his friends are hungry and poor enough to regard any meal as a sacrament; the feast of faith and hope (though not much charity) that is the *vie de Bohème* of the 'twenties happened in fact and, held in memory, can happen again and again like a potent liturgy, revivifying a present that, paradoxically, is well fed but empty of nourishment. Hemingway does not spin a cocoon of affection indifferently round those far days: he remembers certain personages with ruthless dislike and a bitter turn of phrase – Wyndham Lewis's eyes are those of an 'unsuccessful rapist' (Lewis wrote a scornful essay on Hemingway, making him a 'dumb ox'), Ford Madox Ford is 'an ambulatory, well clothed, up-ended hogshead', Gertrude Stein 'was damned nice before she got ambitious'. Scott Fitzgerald comes in for the greatest censure and the most detailed treatment – even the size of his penis become the theme of a brief sketch – and, at the end, he is rubbed out unmercifully:

Many years later at the Ritz bar, long after the end of World War II, Georges, who is the bar chief now and who was the *chasseur* when Scott lived in Paris, asked me, 'Papa, who was this Monsieur Fitzgerald that everyone asks me about?' . . .

'He wrote two very good books and one which was not completed which those who know his writing best say would have been very good. . . .'

'It is strange that I have no memory of him,' Georges said.

But the book is not merely an exercise in destruction. Joyce is remembered with admiration and Pound with affection. And the city itself holds Hemingway's love:

When we came back to Paris it was clear and cold and lovely. The city had accommodated itself to winter, there was good wood for sale at the wood and coal place across our street, and there were braziers outside of many of the good cafés so that you could keep warm on the terraces. Our own apartment was warm and cheerful. We burned *boulets*, which were moulded, egg-shaped lumps of coal dust, on the wood fire, and on the streets the winter light was beautiful. Now you were accustomed to see the bare trees against the sky and you walked on the fresh-washed gravel paths through the Luxembourg gardens in the clear sharp wind. The trees were sculpture without their leaves when you were reconciled to them, and the winter winds blew across the surfaces of the ponds and the fountains blew in the bright light. All the distances were short now since we had been in the mountains.

The prose is pure Hemingway, simple and very evocative, life-accepting but, as always in his work, touched by melancholy. The melancholy resides in the very shape of the sentences which, always avoiding the periodic, cannot resist a dying fall. The Hemingway tune is elegiac even when it most celebrates joy:

There is never any ending to Paris and the memory of each person who has lived in it differs from that of any other. We always returned to it no matter who we were or how it was changed or with what difficulties, or ease, it could be reached. Paris was always worth it and you received return for whatever you brought to it. But this is how Paris was in the early days when we were poor and very happy.

The Hemingway tune was a new and original contribution to world literature. It is in the ears of all young people who set out to write. And the Hemingway code of courage, the Hemingway hero and his stoic holding on against odds, have exerted an influence beyond literature. Though the insufficiencies of the man eventually maimed his work, Hemingway at his best is a seminal force as considerable as that of Joyce or Faulkner or Scott Fitzgerald. And even at his worst he reminds us that to engage literature one has first to engage life.

Dates refer to year of first publication

BOOKS ABOUT
ERNEST HEMINGWAY

BIOGRAPHY:
Baker, Carlos: *Ernest Hemingway, a Life Story*, 1969
Callaghan, Morley: *That Summer in Paris*, 1963
Hemingway, Leicester: *My Brother, Ernest Hemingway*, 1963
Hemingway, Mary: *How It Was*, 1976
Hotchner, A.E.: *Papa Hemingway*, 1966
Loeb, Harold: *The Way it Was*, 1959
Ross, Lillian: *Portrait of Hemingway*, 1950

CRITICISM:
Baker, Carlos: *Hemingway. the Writer as Artist*, 1963
Benson, Jackson J.: *Hemingway; the Writer's Art of Self-Defence*, 1969
Hovey, Richard B.: *Hemingway. the Inward Terrain*, 1969
Rovit, Earl: *Ernest Hemingway*, 1963
Sanderson, Stewart: *Hemingway*, 1963
Stephens, Robert O.: *Hemingway's Non-Fiction. the Public Voice*, 1968
Waldhorn, Arthur: *A Reader's Guide to Ernest Hemingway*, 1972
Watts, Emily: *Ernest Hemingway and the Arts*, 1971
Young, Philip: *Ernest Hemingway. A Reconsideration*, 1966

ESSAYS
Baker, Carlos (ed.): *Hemingway and His Critics*, 1961
Brooks, Cleanth: 'Ernest Hemingway, Man on His Moral Uppers', in *The Hidden God*, 1963, pp. 6–21
Kazin, Alfred: *On Native Grounds*, 1942, pp. 192–204
O'Faolain, Sean: *The Vanishing Hero. Studies in Novelists of the Twenties*, 1956, pp. 112–45
Wilson, Edmund: 'Hemingway, Gauge of Morale', in *The Wound and the Bow*, 1941

OTHER BOOKS
Collins, Larry and Lapierre, Dominique: *Is Paris Burning?*, 1965
Ellman, Richard: *James Joyce*, 1959
Meyers, Jeffrey: *Married to Genius*, 1977
R. Phelps and P. Deane: *The Literary Life*, 1969
Stein, Gertrude: *The Autobiography of Alice B. Toklas*, 1933
Turnbull, Andrew: *Scott Fitzgerald*, 1962

BOOKS BY
ERNEST HEMINGWAY
Three Stories and Ten Poems, 1923
in our time, 1924
In Our Time, 1925
The Torrents of Spring, 1926
The Sun Also Rises (British title, *Fiesta*), 1926
Men Without Women, 1927

A Farewell to Arms, 1929
Death in the Afternoon, 1932
Winner Take Nothing, 1933
Green Hills of Africa, 1935
To Have and Have Not, 1937
The Fifth Column and the First Forty-Nine Stories, 1938
For Whom the Bell Tolls, 1940
Across the River and Into the Trees, 1950
The Old Man and the Sea, 1952

The following were published posthumously:

Fiction
The Fifth Column and Four Stories of the Spanish Civil War, 1969
Islands in the Stream, 1970

Non-fiction
The Wild Years (articles written for the *Toronto Star*), 1962
A Moveable Feast, 1964
By-Line: Ernest Hemingway, Selected Articles and Despatches of Four Decades, edited by William White, 1967
Ernest Hemingway: Cub Reporter, Kansas City Star Stories, edited by M. Bruccoli, 1970
Ernest Hemingway's Apprenticeship, Oak Park, 1916–17, edited by M. Bruccoli, 1971

1899   Born 21 July at Oak Park near Chicago, second child of Dr Clarence E. Hemingway and Grace Hall.

1917   After graduation at Oak Park High School, Hemingway joins the *Kansas City Star* as a junior reporter.

1918   Barred by defective vision from joining the armed forces in the Great War which the United States has just entered, he enrols with the Red Cross as an ambulance driver. Sent to Italy, he is wounded on the Piave front while performing an act of rescue. In hospital in Milan he falls in love with a nurse, Agnes von Kurowsky. Decorated for bravery under fire by both Italian and U.S. Governments.

1919   Returns to Oak Park, fêted as a war hero. Restless, chided by his mother for indolence, he starts writing seriously but without commercial success.

1920   Joins the *Toronto Star*. Later edits a periodical published in Chicago. Marries Hadley Richardson and, in December, goes with her to Paris as European correspondent of the *Toronto Star*.

1923   His first son is born. *Three Stories and Ten Poems* is published in Paris.

1924   Publishes *in our time*, again in Paris. The book is favourably noticed by Edmund Wilson. Assists Ford Madox Ford on the *transatlantic review*.

1925   *In Our Time*, his first commercial publication, meets critical approval in America.

1926   Publishes *The Torrents of Spring*, an ill-natured satire on the fictional style of his friend Sherwood Anderson. In October, *The Sun Also Rises* (*Fiesta* in Britain) has a great commercial as well as critical success.

1927   *Men Without Women*, a volume of stories, confirms Hemingway's importance. He divorces Hadley.

1928   He marries Pauline Pfeiffer and returns with her to America. He sets up house for the first time on his native soil at Key West, Florida. His second son is born, and Pauline's difficult *accouchement* is recorded in *A Farewell to Arms*. His father, incurably ill, commits suicide.

1929   *A Farewell to Arms* is published.

1932   *Death in the Afternoon*, a book about bullfighting. Hemingway is taken to task by writers of the Left for avoiding in his work the major political and economic issues of the period of the Depression.

1933   *Winner Take Nothing*.

1935   *Green Hills of Africa*.

1937   *To Have and Have Not* seeks to satisfy the Leftist critics by presenting the problems of a free individual in a corrupt society dominated by money.

1937   Hemingway is in Spain as a journalist, but his sympathies with the Popular Front and his enmity towards Franco are made apparent by his work on the film *The Spanish Earth*.

1938   He publishes his pro-Republican play *The Fifth Column* at the head of his volume of collected stories, which include 'Francis Macomber' and 'The Snows of Kilimanjaro', fine fruits of his African safaris.

1940   He marries Martha Gellhorn, a fellow-journalist with whom his friendship ripened in Spain. His house in Florida having been deeded to Pauline, he settles in Cuba.

For Whom the Bell Tolls is immensely popular, but the critics murmur about a falling off of literary standards.

1941   Hemingway and Martha go to the Far East to write articles on the Sino-Japanese War. With America's entry into the Second World War, Hemingway runs his own 'Q-ship' off the Cuban coast.

1944   He goes to Europe as a war correspondent, takes part in the Normandy invasion, enters Paris with his own partisan unit. There is trouble about his violating his non-combatant status, but eventually he is awarded the Bronze Star.

1945   In love with the journalist Mary Welsh, he is divorced by Martha.

1946   He marries Mary, his fourth and last wife, and starts work on a fictional saga about the earth, the sea, and the air.

1948   In Italy, he gathers the materials for:

1950   *Across the River and Into the Trees*. The response to the novel is poor. Hemingway recovers his reputation with:

1952   *The Old Man and the Sea*. This work has a tremendous impact on millions of readers.

1953   He is awarded the Pulitzer Prize.

1954   He is awarded the Nobel Prize. He regrets his inability to go to Stockholm to receive it in person, pleading the aftermath of concussion suffered in two successive plane crashes in Africa. Actually he is suffering a general physical and nervous degeneration.

1960   At work on a lengthy study of bullfighting called *The Dangerous Summer*, part of which is published in *Life*. Also he is putting together a volume of reminiscences of Paris entitled *A Moveable Feast*. Sick, he goes to a clinic in Minnesota.

1961   At Ketchum in Idaho, Cuba being too unstable a country to live in during the early days of the Castro takeover. His sickness grows despite skilled treatment. Physically etiolated, profoundly psychotic, he commits suicide on 2 July.

LIST OF ILLUSTRATIONS

3200P in the John F. Kennedy Library.

99 Adriana Ivancich. Photo No. E H 3697P in the John F. Kennedy Library.

101 Dust jackets of the first American editions of *Across the River and Into the Trees* and *The Old Man and the Sea*. Charles Scribner's Sons.

102 Hemingway and Mary on safari in the 1950s. Photo No. E H 8463P in the John F. Kennedy Library.

103 Hemingway with Philip Percival on safari. Photo No. E H 2730P in the John F. Kennedy Library.

103 The plane after the crash in Kenya. Photo No. E H 2988P in the John F. Kennedy Library.

104 Ava Gardner. Photo Culver Pictures.

105 Ingrid Bergman. Photo Culver Pictures.

107 Hemingway. Photo Popperfoto.

108 Hemingway with Fidel Castro, 1960. Photo Camera Press.

109 Hemingway at Yesa Dam, near Pamplona, 1959. Photo Camera Press.

111 The house at Ketchum, Idaho. Photo No. E H 2193P in the John F. Kennedy Library.

113 Hemingway at Ketchum. Photo No. E H 2923P in the John F. Kennedy Library.

INDEX